Cyrille's Talk

Building a Culture of Compassion in the Catholic High School (and every other high school on the planet)

DANNY BROCK
CYRILLE SANTOS

RESOURCE *Publications* · Eugene, Oregon

CYRILLE'S TALK
Building a Culture of Compassion in the Catholic High School (and every other high school on the planet)

Resource Publications
An Imprint of Wipf and Stock Publishers
199 W. 8th Ave., Suite 3
Eugene, OR 97401

www.wipfandstock.com

PAPERBACK ISBN: 978-1-6667-1982-6
HARDCOVER ISBN: 978-1-6667-1983-3
EBOOK ISBN: 978-1-6667-1984-0

09/07/21

Scripture cited in the Introduction is from The Jerusalem Bible, Readers Edition, c 1968 by Darton, Longman & Todd Ltd and Doubleday & Company, Inc.

All other Scripture quotations contained herein are from the New Revised Standard Version Bible: Catholic Edition copyright c 1993 and 1989 by the Division of Christian Education of the National Council of the Churches of Christ in the U.S.A. Used by permission. All rights reserved.

Cyrille is pronounced SIGH (as in exhaling a deep audible breath expressing sorrow with a hint of longing) and RILL rhymes with 'hill' (an elevated piece of land; once ascended, you can see a great distance) SIGH-RILL, Cyrille!

Thank you to Gemma Knott for technical assistance on the manuscript. The right person, with the right skills, for the right job, at the right time.

I, Danny, would like to thank the following teachers I was fortunate to work with, over the years, in the formation of student leadership retreat teams:
Sandy Burgardt
Debbie Moses
Cathy Fowlie
Corinne Ballam

This book is dedicated to Bishop Gary Gordon and the priests and deacons and the women and men religious of the Diocese of Victoria, British Columbia, Canada. In thanksgiving for your loving service to Vancouver Islanders.

All the self-help books and all the good advice
about learning to love myself
and finding the reassurance within
don't seem to get to the root of the longing:
to be sure that someone in my life will stay with me.
That if I let myself love another human being
and let myself trust,
I won't be abandoned.
That I'll be safe.
And that when I reach out, the person I love will still be there
and will be reaching back toward me.[1]

ELIZABETH KIM
TEN THOUSAND SORROWS

Contents

Introduction

This book begins with a talk given by a high school student, Cyrille Santos, on her grade 12 retreat at Saint Andrew's Regional Catholic High School, in Victoria, British Columbia, Canada.

It continues with an explanation of how student-led retreats and religious education classes can build a culture of compassion in the Catholic high school.

The Catholic school, like so much else in our culture, can get busy with many things. We can end up polishing our image while neglecting our soul. We can spin off in so many directions and abandon the core of who we are.

> A Catholic school, therefore, cannot be a factory for the learning of various skills and competencies designed to fill the echelons of business and industry. Nor is it for "clients" and "consumers" in a competitive marketplace that values academic achievement. Education is not a commodity, even if Catholic schools equip their graduates with enviable skills. Rather, "the Catholic school sets out to be a school for the human person and of human persons."[2]

The above quote is from *The Holy See's Teaching on Catholic Schools*, by Archbishop J. Michael Miller, CSB, a resource liberally cited throughout this book.

This book proposes that a school "for the human person and of human persons" is a school with a culture of compassion.

In Jesus' final discourse to his disciples he told them to love others as he has loved them. The experience of being loved, as Jesus loved, is the only foundation of faith that lasts. The biggest influence on a person's life is the quality of love they experience, not the religious tradition they are raised with. Students need to receive the gift of their own goodness in order to trust the goodness of God. The seed of faith grows in the soil of love.

People whose life experience is devoid of love and compassion either forsake religion altogether or develop a religiosity that is stone hearted, stiff necked, fearful and prone to intolerance and violence in its many forms. If the experience of love and compassion gives birth to healthy religion, then the Catholic school should be a place where students experience love and compassion. There are things we must do to make this happen. We must have student-led retreats and we must have religion classes that tend to the soul-struggles of youth. How to do this is the subject of this book.

What can be said of the church, Ecclesia semper reformanda est—The church must always be reformed, can also be said of the Catholic school.

There are critics who lament the decreasing Catholic identity (catholicity) in our Catholic schools. Some say it is the presence of non-Catholics and people with no religion (nones). Some say it is the ever encroaching effect of secularization.

It is neither.

The problem is not with 'them', but with us. The solution is in how we engage our students—all of them.

Adults and adolescents, working together, can build a culture of compassion in the school. This is the reform the high school needs. This is the core of our catholicity. And this is what high school students long for.

Pope Benedict XVI, in his encyclical letter, Deus Caritas Est, God is Love, tells us that Jesus came to give us "a heart which sees. This heart sees where love is needed and acts accordingly."

This book shows how religious educators and retreat directors can have a "heart which sees." Anonymous pre-and-post student retreat evaluation forms, quoted extensively in this book, show "where love is needed," and where the Catholic school can "act accordingly."

If you only surf through this book and read these student comments you will gain a greater capacity to see with your heart. All excerpts from student evaluation forms are *italicized* as with the following:

> *I really appreciate the effort you put into retreats . . . and helping your students keep in touch with the important things in life. I also appreciate how you read each individual evaluation that you get back. It makes me feel like my opinion really counts.*

I, Danny, met a student who graduated from our high school. By self definition he was non-religious. He said to me, "The one thing I learned from St. Andrew's is to have compassion for other people."

Be compassionate as your Father is compassionate. Luke 6:36

This is a book to help adults:

- direct youth retreats
- teach teens religion
- administer high schools
- parent teenagers

It will also help teenagers imagine the kind of high school where they are the young church of today and not just the church of the future.

This book promotes the idea that an authentic Catholic high school is one that builds a culture of compassion. This book is a how-to and a why-to, but it is also a taste of what awaits you, should you accept this mission. Few things are sweeter than sincere and unsolicited words of thanks from the grateful heart of a teenager.

Chapters 1 and 3 are written by Cyrille; chapters 2, 4, 5 are written by Danny.

Front Matter Endnotes

1. Kim, *Ten Thousand Sorrows*, 219–220.
2. Miller, *The Holy See's Teaching*, 24.

1

Cyrille's Talk

"All sorrows can be borne if you put them into a
story or tell a story about them."

—ISAK DINESEN

I was born into a very religious family. I'm Filipino, which means Catholicism is in my blood. You could say I was a Cultural Catholic. As a kid, my faith wasn't really part of me, it was just something I felt I had to do because everyone else did.

In grade eight I was in Catholic high school and part of a Catholic youth group. I attended retreats and met new people with the same faith. Even with these new experiences, I still felt my faith was just something I was born with, or something I had to do. One thing I found difficult was balancing my faith with secular society— trying to fit in but also do what I think is right or what I believe.

In grade nine I started to be more self aware, thinking more about who I was. When it came to faith I felt it more as "peer pressure" in a way. I had to be religious because my friends and family were. I started copying others in my youth group trying to be religious like them and pretending to have a relationship with God like them. I did this to try to fit in, but what happened is I soon became labeled as the "Christian Girl," a holy church goer.

Some of my classmates said they couldn't swear around me or do certain things around me. They would say things like, "Cyrille can't go here because she has to go to church and she only hangs around with her church friends." This bothered me.

One thing that I wanted and waited for at this time in my life, was a special moment, what I called a spark, an experience of God that would make my faith strong. I would always hear talks about how this grand moment changed their lives and made them closer to God. And I was always waiting for my miracle to happen.

And then came grade ten.

Two of my closest friends left for a different school, and I felt all alone and didn't belong anywhere. I compared myself to other people and felt there was something wrong with me. I have an older sister and she was smarter, prettier and more talented than me and she had so many friends. I love my sister and we have a very good relationship but I just felt like I was comparing myself to a standard I could never reach. Grade ten was a really sad and lonely point in my life.

All these feelings I had, I kept to myself and told no one, not even my closest friends. I thought that no one cared or that I wasn't important enough to be heard. Because I bottled everything up, there were times I would go to the bathroom, cry, and let it all out. During lunch, when I would feel lonely, I would sit in the bathroom and just cry and get angry with God. I would rant to God saying, "Why am I in the bathroom?" Or, "Why am I feeling so lonely? I go to church. I try to be a good person. Why am I feeling this way?" This lasted throughout grade ten and was the lowest point in high school.

Then the summer came and I started hanging out with my friends who were not from my school. I started to change by trying to become more like them. They did not influence me to change, I just thought I had to be like them to be worthy of their friendship. Before I did anything I thought: What would they do? Or, do they like what I am doing? I tried so hard to change myself and become like my friends. It was painful to try to please them, to try to fit in and to constantly change myself to be like them. I knew what I was doing was wrong. It was tiring to try so hard to be like them. I spent a lot of time in my room, lonely and disappointed in myself.

During this time at home during the summer, I still continued to question God, always telling God how I felt. I thought to myself: "At least someone's there to listen."

With grade eleven starting, I wanted a new start. I was tired of being lonely and tired of feeling pain in my heart. I wanted to try new things. I tried to keep a healthy distance with my friends, knowing that I needed to do things on my own.

I challenged myself to get more involved with school. I was in student council, which helped me grow out of my comfort zone. I reached out to other students. I started to help with school liturgies and got more involved with the drama department. I joined new clubs and started talking to new people. I enjoyed all these things, and even though I still felt lonely and in pain, I was able to find ways to deal with these feelings and not dwell in the sad and dark place. The pain I felt throughout grade ten, and during the summer, motivated me to find happiness in myself.

Now, I am happy to say, I am in a different place. To this day, I don't know why these things happened to me or what caused them. When I look back I see good times when I was strong in my faith, sad times when I questioned my faith, and even times where I thought I could leave and forget my faith. My parents never forced me, which would make it easier to just leave. I thought that if I left, what would I do and who would I turn to. If I wasn't talking to God, I would consider myself crazy, because I would just be talking to myself all the time.

I have decided to continue on with this journey of faith because I believe there is a reason behind all this pain I am feeling.

It also helps me to know that there is always Someone there for me—to listen, to rant to, to talk to, or even to blame when things go wrong. Knowing this has helped me through this dark place, because who knows what I could have done or what would have happened to me if I didn't know Someone was always there for me.

I was always afraid of expressing my faith and standing firm in what I believe in, but look at me now, I am here in front of you sharing my journey with God.

I challenge you to think about where you are right now in your journey. Whether you're in a really dark place, or a happy place. Wherever you are, embrace it.

2

A Letter to Cyrille

"When I meet God I want to ask him about the
mystery of suffering, I do not understand it at all."

—Romano Guardini, Theologian, author of *The Lord*

Dear Cyrille,

Thank you for your talk. You spoke the truth: to God, to your-self, and to us. It was a truth hewn from experience and forged in the furnace of pain.

When you spoke the truth to God in your complaints, in your questions and in your rants, you were connecting with God, though God seemed far away and unresponsive. You shared the truth of your life—what you were thinking and how you were feeling. You were going through a 'dark night of the soul'.

You evoked sadness in me and those who heard your talk as you described the pain you felt, alone, in the bathroom, in tears. When you shared your feelings with us, you shared your very self. In doing so, we came to know you and you experienced be-ing known. It took courage to open yourself like you did, and you were received with gratitude and affection. Your talk gave others courage to look with honesty at their own life journey. As your talk helped students at Saint Andrew's High School, I believe it can help students elsewhere.

Cyrille, in your talk you said your faith in grade eight and nine felt like "peer pressure," having to be religious "because my friends and family were." You copied others "trying to be religious like them." Then you asked God to give you real faith—a spark, a grand moment, a miracle, something other people said happened to them. But, instead, you were plunged into a dark night of sorrow and loneliness.

Cyrille, you said, "To this day I do not know why this happened to me."

All of your talk, and particularly this question—why?, expresses the 'holy longing' of your soul. As a religion teacher I would like to offer some thoughts and reflections that your talk has prompted in me. Thank you for permitting me to walk a few steps with you along the sacred path of your life.

> Don't waste your time dreaming of being someone else.
> Don't try to be someone else. Work and pray at being yourself.
> St. Francis de Sales

Cyrille, when you were in grade nine and you wanted God to give you real faith, a spark, a grand moment—who were 'You'? Back then, the 'you' that you wanted God to give faith to, was not the real and authentic you, but the want-to-be-someone-else you. It's as if God were to say: I want to give you faith, but I don't recognize you anymore. I don't want your imitation of someone else. I want you.

In theology it has been said: Grace builds on Nature. Grace is God's miracle, God's spark, God's grand moment. Nature is our human nature, our growth in becoming who we really are. The interplay of grace and nature is a great mystery. All our human attempts to explain this mystery fall short. Some would say the dualistic separation of grace and nature is misleading. I agree. Still, it points to a truth we sense dimly: God working in us and our desire to be authentic is the heart of spirituality. God being God and us being us is what bears fruit. "Comparing yourself to other people," said Saint Teresa of Avila, "is the death of the spiritual life." It's as if God were saying: You want a new faith for an old self. You want new wine for an old wine skin.

> And no one puts new wine into old wineskins; otherwise,
> the wine will burst the skins, and the wine is lost, and so
> are the skins; but one puts new wine into fresh wineskins.
> Mark 2:22

Cyrille, you cried out to God for new wine, but God could not give you new wine because it would burst the old wineskins and the wine would be lost.

Why did this happen to you?

There is one place we should look for an answer. A place called Adolescence.

> You don't have to suffer to be a poet; adolescence is
> enough suffering for anybody.[1]
> John Ciardi

The journey of adolescence is the journey of discovering your true self; the self God created you to be. This true self cannot be found by being like someone else and having a faith like them. Deep down, Cyrille, you knew this.

The agenda of adolescence is to face one's self. Some may say it is to face God. This is true, but true only in light of the words of Saint Augustine. "Grant, Lord, that I may know myself that I may know thee."

Adolescence is a spiritual journey in search of self and in search of God. It is the same search. Notice in your story the two great quests: Who am I? Where is God? These are not two separate paths, they advance together.

> There is only one problem on which all my existence, my
> peace, and my happiness depend: to discover myself in
> discovering God.
>   If I find Him I will find myself and if I find my true
> self I will find Him.[2]
> Thomas Merton

It is tempting to ask God for a way out of the necessary struggle and consequent pain of adolescence. We learn, however, that God does not take us out, but accompanies us through the challenges we face.

Darkness is the winter of the soul, the time when it seems that nothing is growing. But winter, we know, is the fallow time of year. Winter is the time when the earth renews itself. And so it is with struggle. Unbeknownst to us, struggle is the call and the signal that we are about to renew ourselves. Whether we want to or not.[3]

Joan D. Chittister OSB

When one authentically engages their own life, as you did, they have, knowingly or unknowingly, engaged God.

You courageously engaged life when you acknowledged the pain you experienced, called out to God in anguish, argued with God like Job in the Bible and . . . waited. Accepting life is entering into life rather than exiting life, as you hint at the end of your talk: "Who knows what I could have done."

"Knowing God and knowing self are . . . interdependent," says David G. Benner, the author of *The Gift of Being Yourself*. "Neither can proceed very far without the other."[4]

Why is this?

God-knowledge without self-knowledge produces a rootless spirituality that is more an external show than an inward dynamic. Self-knowledge without God-knowledge leads to grandiosity and self-obsession. Looking for yourself 'in God', however, allows you to be both honest with yourself and to see yourself as God sees you—with Love. The short answer is this: God knows us, and to know ourselves as God knows us is a homecoming, coming home to ourselves.

The struggle of adolescence is the struggle of becoming your authentic self. But it is also the struggle of learning how to struggle—how to handle a whirlwind of change, how to stand in a storm of insecurity, how to hear an inner voice while thunder breaks all about, and how to accept and love yourself in a cultural tsunami of competition and comparison. These are the great spiritual tasks of life, and they begin in adolescence. Teenagers need a good beginning.

God loves teenagers and God has a purpose for adolescence. Some parents try to streamline adolescence by putting teens on a fast track to a successful career in business, sports or the arts. Many teens are caught up in the pressure and carry the stress level of a medical intern. Is this what adolescence is about?

The spiritual task of adolescence is to discover God's view of us: You are blessed, you are loved, you are a child of God. It is out of this realization, this energy, that our own life can unfold.

Some adults want to dismiss adolescence as 'just a phase'. But I think we need to view adolescence compassionately—others' adolescence, and our own. If you look compassionately you will see the problem of adolescence as the great problem of life: choosing a false self or a true self, being authentic or a copy, being sincere or wearing a mask.

> The most exhausting thing in life, I have discovered, is being insincere. That is why so much of social life is exhausting; one is wearing a mask. I have shed my mask.[5]
> Anne Morrow Lindbergh

Sincerity is the energy of adolescence. It is God's sustainable energy. Without it we become depleted. Teens fastidiously calculating the social hierarchy in high school and trying to fit in are exhausted. As one teen recalled: "When I came to high school, I had a three step program. First, find out who the popular people are. Second, find out what the popular people like. Third, like what the popular people like."

Your talk, Cyrille, reveals God's sustainable energy in you. Your talk overflows with sincerity. The word sincerity comes from the Latin word "sincerus" which means "uncorrupted." That is why your talk touched the hearts and inspired the students who listened to you. Your talk was authentic as student evaluation forms reveal.

> *The talks were genuine. It makes you realize you are not the only one struggling.*
>
> *The talks were my favorite parts of the whole retreat.*
>
> *Really good to hear and know the stories of our classmates and what they have learned. Amazing experience.*

The talks were enlightening. I do not think the words spoken will fade from memory soon, if at all.

We often don't know our classmates as well as we think we do.

I really enjoyed Cyrille's talk.

In his book, *Will Our Children Have Faith*, John H. Westerhoff outlines the four stages of faith development. He calls the first stage, *Experienced Faith*—the faith development of the pre-born, newborn and primary school student. Religious education begins in the womb with a sense of being loved and welcomed—or not. Newborns inhale their parents' love and absorb trust when their needs are met, developing what Conrad Baars calls a "felt faith," a foundation for religious faith.

The second stage, elementary school, is *Affiliative Faith*, identifying with one's family and one's culture. The body of faith dresses itself in the songs, traditions and rituals of the ethnic community one belongs to. This is the stage you refer to as "Cultural Catholic," being born and raised into a religious family.

The third stage is called *Searching Faith*, the faith development stage of adolescence. Searching faith is the labor pains that give birth to the last stage, *Owned Faith*, the faith of adulthood.

Searching faith begins the process of making faith one's own—a necessary step in keeping faith alive. There is a saying: God has no grandchildren. Our parents chose faith for us, now we must choose it for ourselves. We must choose to be daughters and sons of God in our own right. The cognitive development that marks adolescence brings new questions about God, and, in the process, may shatter previous ideas we have about God, the most common being: If one has faith they are spared trouble in life. The faith pains of your adolescence, Cyrille, is proof to the contrary.

Cyrille, it might seem strange, but you were "becoming yourself" when you thought you were most "beside yourself." When you were in pain, and called it by name, and cried out to God—that is when you were most becoming yourself. You say, "I started to become more aware." It bothered you when others stereotyped you,

"Christian girl," because you knew, in your heart, that real faith is not a label in someone else's head but an adventure within one's own life. Such discernment and self awareness in grade eight and nine beautifully reveals the journey from *Affiliative Faith* to *Searching Faith*. This life process that you courageously engaged, is God's very life working within you. You were distraught, and reduced to the core of yourself. Yet your dark night was a crucible where the death of trying to be like others gave way to a resurrection of a newly discovered budding self, your very own new wine skin.

The transition from one stage of faith to another can be painful. We can feel lost, shaken, insecure. Yet, beneath the soil of our life, something is growing.

Cyrille, something else strikes me as to why this happened to you.

It happened because you asked for a miracle. You asked for a spark, a grand moment, your own miracle to happen. I believe it did.

The miracle you were asking for came disguised as a dark night. Your grand moment did not happen to you, your grand moment happened within you. God did not come from the outside in, God came from the inside out. God did not send the dark night, but God was in it with you.

This understanding, that God does not will our suffering, is an area of confusion for many people of faith today. But confusion here imperils our faith journey.

> Is there anyone among you who, if your child asks for bread, will give a stone? Or if the child asks for a fish, will give a snake? If you then, who are evil, know how to give good gifts to your children, how much more will your Father in heaven give good things to those who ask him.
> Matthew 7:9–11

God, the Father, gives what is good. God does not will our suffering. To my students I explain it this way: God did not take you grandfather. Death took your grandfather, and God is going to take your grandfather from death. This I learned from a marvelous book called *Good Goats, Healing our Image of God* by Dennis, Sheila and Matthew Linn.

Jesuit author, Peter van Breemen, writes in his book, *The God Who Won't Let Go*: "The Father did not "will" the death of His Son (Jesus). It had to happen according to the terrible logic of this world as we have shaped it."[6] In traditional Christian theology this "terrible logic" is referred to as Original Sin. Our life, as we experience it, is broken and wounded. We are fearful, insecure and self-negating. The word sin originally meant "missing the mark," and that describes how we feel about our self—we missed!

But this is not God's doing or God's plan. God's plan is abundant life (John 10:10). Before original sin there was an original blessing when all was "good" and humans "very good" (Genesis 1:31). God is the answer to our problems, not the cause of them.

> Out of the divine plenitude God loves those who suffer,
> shares their pain, and bears their burdens with them.[7]
> Ilia Delio

God does not send us suffering but shares the suffering with us. Although this is a crucial truth to hold on to, it does not solve what is called the "problem of pain": If God is all powerful, why does God allow our personal suffering and monumental historical suffering.

This is a huge stone blocking the spiritual path for many. This is the stone that sealed Lazarus. This is the stone at the tomb of Jesus. "Who will move the stone for us?," asked the women as they journeyed to the grave on Easter Sunday. This is the question you asked Cyrille, and it is the question we all ask, at one time, in our life.

The problem of pain is a mystery to live more than a problem to solve. In his own suffering Jesus cried out: My God, My God, why have you abandoned me. Mark. W. Baker, the author of *Spiritual Wisdom for a Happier Life*, helps us understand that when Jesus cried these words, it was not a lack of faith, it was trauma, the psychological state of feeling isolated by others and abandoned by God. This is how you felt in grade ten. Jesus felt it too.

In the Gospel account, Jesus prays: Father, into your hands I commit my Spirit. Into your hands, O Lord, is how we live the mystery of suffering. In the midst of suffering, Jesus prayed. And, Cyrille, so did you.

Cyrille, when you called out to God, that was prayer. That was a sign of God-within-you. Prayer is initiated by God who dwells in our heart. Prayer helps us handle the fact that we can't handle the fact. Mostly, prayer works on us rather than for us. "Prayer," writes van Breeman, "is God-at-work-in-us."[8] Our response in prayer is being receptive to what God is doing.

> When you search for me, you will find me; if you seek me with all your heart, I will let you find me, says the Lord . . .
> Jeremiah 29: 13–14

Here is where I see God-with-you in your story:

- You were not content to live a peer pressured faith. You wanted an authentic faith, not just a hand-me-down, or hand-me-over faith.

- You discovered that trying to be like others results in disliking yourself. You wanted to be your true self.

- And in the midst of what you experienced as God's painful silence, with no apparent spark to ignite a miracle, you still kept telling God how you felt. You still believed that "at least someone's there to listen."

This is God-at-work-with-you.

"God comes to you," writes Paula D'Arcy, "disguised as your life."[9]

God is closer to us than we are to ourselves. Adolescence is the journey of trying to get close to ourselves. When we do, there is God. God was calling you all the time, calling you home. The grand moment did not come as a mighty wind storm and a great earthquake. It came as a still small voice within you, and you listened (1 Kings 19:11).

You might think, but I didn't hear any "voices" within me! When God speaks to us in the depths of our heart, God speaks to us using our own voice. You gave God permission to do so when you called out to God from your heart. That is what scripture is as well—God's message in human words. Without faith we only see human words, with faith we begin to see God's message. In grade eleven, when you said to yourself, "I want a new start, I'm tired of being lonely, of feeling pain in my heart, I want to try new things," whose words were these? Yours, of course. And God's. They were inspired words that came from your deep heart where God resides.

In his book *Wrestling with God*, Ronald Rolheiser, O.M.I., notes that God's presence in our life is mostly quiet and hidden. He writes: "Simply put, God lies inside us, deep inside, but in a way that's almost non-existent, almost unfelt, largely unnoticed, and easily ignored."

But the presence calls to us, Rolheiser explains, and invites us to draw from it like a well. "And, if we do draw upon it, it gushes up in us in an infinite stream that instructs us, nurtures us, and fills us with endless energy."[10] That, Cyrille, is what God is doing in you.

It seems God's spark and grand-moment-miracles come, mostly, in barely audible whispers, and sometimes in the kind of silence that speaks. I believe, Cyrille, that it was intimacy with God that you sought when you asked for a grand moment. And I believe God is showing you a new path to that intimacy. Afterall, it is not so much a sign of the existence of God that we seek, but an experience of God's closeness. Perhaps, in the great scheme of things, God did not give you what you asked for because God has something better in mind.

One of the reasons why we do not think of God as being within us, is because we are so used to thinking of God as beyond us. Yet God is both. In theology we speak of God's transcendence—God is beyond anything we can imagine; and God's immanence—God is closer to us than we are to ourselves. Both descriptions of God point to a beyond and a beneath that is outside our ability to grasp completely. All our talk of God is but a human approximation, for God cannot be "captured" with human words derived from human thought. Still, becoming more aware of the immanence of God reminds us of what is most important: God loves us, and abides in us and seeks intimacy with us.

Your ranting to God was not a sign of your rejection of God, but a sign of your belief in God's love. Apathy is the opposite of love, and apathetic people don't rant, they just don't care.

Complaining to God is also a sign that your relationship to God is important to you. Saint Teresa of Avila, as the story goes, after being tossed by her horse into a mudhole, complained out loud to God, saying, "If this is the way you treat your friends, no wonder you have so few." Complaining to God, being real with God, is one way we nurture our relationship with God. The love God gives us makes us free to complain.

Cyrille, you did not fall into a momentary mud hole. Your mud hole lasted a whole year. There is an allegory I read some years ago. A person fell into a deep dark pit. So deep and so dark that when she looked up she saw only the faintest pinpoint of light from where she had fallen. She tried to climb the sides of the pit to get to the light, but it was too steep. Trying again and again with no success, she fell to the ground in despair.

Looking around she noticed that there was one corner of the pit that was the darkest of all. The faint light could not breach it. She avoided this corner afraid she would lose sight of the only light she could see. So there she sat, in the pit, in deepening despair. Finally, after many hours, she stood up and walked into the dark corner. It is hopeless just to do nothing, she thought, what have I to lose? In the dark corner she could see nothing, not even her own hands that groped the steep sides of the pit. But, after a while, as she groped along in the darkness, she realized she was no longer in a pit but in a winding narrow tunnel. Though tempted to turn back, to that faint light she knew, she journeyed on with a determination and resolve that surprised herself. And in time, time she could not gauge or calculate, the tunnel led her to the opening of a cave, from which she emerged, into the bright light of a glorious spring day.

Cyrille, the person in this story is you.

You kept looking for ways to be like others, to be worthy of their friendship, even though to do so was tiring, painful, and as you knew, unhealthy. But it was, at that time, the only faint light you saw. You didn't know that the real light was in the darkness.

In another way, the faint light you saw was your faith as you understood it at the time. In the dim light of that faith you kept asking: Why is this happening to me, why am I in a dark pit? Was it time for your faith to be reborn? A rebirth that must remain, for a while, in the darkness of the womb. Was the painful experience not the loss of faith but the labor pains of new born faith. It was the darkest corner of your life where deliverance was found. It was out of the darkness of a tomb that Jesus rose.

Thomas Moore, author of *Dark Nights of the Soul*, writes: "If you give all your effort to getting rid of your dark night, you may not learn its lessons or go through the important changes it can make for you." The dark times he says "leave their mark and make you a person of insight and compassion."[11]

Some people who go through a dark night don't tell anyone. In a way, they don't tell themselves. They think sad is bad and vulnerability is weakness. Their secret becomes a shameful secret. But this shame stands in the way of the development of their true self. They need to tell their story. They need someone to hear their story with love and compassion. God can help us take every experience in our life, and use it for our own transformation. In the economy of God's grace, nothing is wasted.

> At the very center of your life, you are linked to God, and the storms and floods will come, but they will not destroy you.[12]
> Bishop Robert Barron

Cyrille, I find your talk so compelling because you have given teenage expression to the great dilemma of faith expressed in Jacob's wrestling with an angel—God in disguise (Genesis 32) and Job's "The Lord gives, the Lord takes away, blessed be the name of the Lord" (Job 1:21). In our own times we have C.S. Lewis's *A Grief Observed*; Philip Yancey's, *Where is God when it Hurts*; Joan Chittister's, *Scarred by Struggle, Transformed by Hope*; Ronald Rolheiser's, *Wrestling with God*; Harold Kushner's, *When Bad Things Happen to Good People*, and many other authors who pray and ponder this perennial dilemma.

Yet, alongside these testimonies of claiming faith in darkness, there are others who, similarly afflicted, see only an empty and appallingly silent abyss.

I must say, I don't blame them. I can't blame them. I have not suffered as they have. And if such a trial ever came my way, I can only hope I would subsist in faith. But if such a cup were to be passed to me, I would pray it were passed away.

We stand in faith with a great multitude from every nation (Revelation 7:9), what we call the Communion of Saints. And yet, too, we stand alone. Faith is both glamorously public, and fiercely personal. Before anyone's struggling journey of faith, we need to bow in reverence and awe. And we should be slow, very slow, to judge someone we think has "lost" faith.

> There are few things as isolating as suffering. Everyone's suffering is largely incommunicable. . . . Overall, the struggles you face about almost any part of your life are so private, so personal and so unique, that even when you do explain them you may feel that you've given someone the wrong impression.
> But there is one person who understands you fully: the Risen Christ.
> James Martin, SJ[13]

Less than a century ago a singular evil unfolded on the planet. What Jews call the Shoah (calamity in Hebrew) and others the Holocaust, fell upon the people of the Covenant.

When Rabbi Irving Greenberg was young he met survivors of the Shoah. He then studied "the calamity" intensely. And then he lost his faith—in a way. The darkness of the Shoah seemed all consuming. "Now, how can one go on speaking of God or the value of human life in that kind of world?" he asked himself. The absence of God tormented him for years. Restoration of faith began with a sense of loyalty to his fellow Jews who died for their faith; was enlivened by the birth of his son; and then by a revelation that came to him after the anger and rage: "I began to feel a certain pity for God, and a certain compassion that God was suffering."

Rabbi Greenberg came to the realization that the "all-powerful, omnipotent God" that religious people are raised to believe in, is a correct image. It is especially helpful in the first stage of our relationship with God. This image of God affirms that we are "plugged into this infinite source of life, and it is going to grow."[14]

And, yet, the image of a suffering God is also correct. The rabbi felt compassion for the one who is Compassion and realized that the partnership between the divine and the human is to pour compassion on the wounds of this suffering world.

God suffers with us. And together, in partnership (the biblical covenant) we minister to others and all of creation. As if God was saying: Cyrille, we made it through, let's continue to journey together and accompany others who struggle with the problem of pain.

And that is what you did, Cyrille, when you sat before eighty five students and gave your talk. Perhaps we can't help anyone unless we drink from the cup they are drinking from. God knows the taste of our suffering.

Your talk helped others to be honest with God, as you were, and to persevere on the journey, as you did.

3

Cyrille's Response

"Let your religion be less of a theory and more of a
love affair."

—G. K. CHESTERTON

It has been a few years now since I graduated from high school and
I am about halfway through my bachelor's degree at the University
of Victoria.

Coming from a very small and close-knit community at St.
Andrew's high school, I was nervous to venture off into the "real
world" and start university. I went to high school with the same
people I went to elementary school with, so, in a way, this was my
first experience going to a new school. I loved being involved in
many clubs at St. Andrew's and getting to know the staff and students. I loved how everything was so familiar to me, so going to
university, where I knew hardly anybody, terrified me. Another aspect that I was scared to lose was the sense of community within the
Catholic faith. As I've said, I've grown up in a Catholic household
and went to a Catholic school my whole life. This was truly the first
time where I faced life outside a Catholic community, in a secular
world. This really challenged my faith.

Going to university, not having retreats and not being in a
Catholic environment scared me at first because I thought it would

make me "lose" my faith. Because of this fear, I actively sought out a Catholic community. I heard of an organization called Catholic Christian Outreach (CCO), and I knew it was at the university, so I immediately wanted to get involved. I was so used to the Catholic community at high school and wanted to find the same thing at university. During my first week I eagerly looked for CCO at Clubs Day, and I signed up to get involved. It was so nice and heart-warming to be surrounded by like-minded Catholics again. Because I was missing retreats and the Catholic environment at Saint Andrew's, I really made an effort to stay connected with the people in CCO.

Having retreats and going to a Catholic high school really helped me realize my true calling: to be in relationship and community with other Catholics. Finding a Catholic community at university strengthened my faith and helped me make my faith my own, something more personal. It strengthened my desire to want God in my life and this led to wonder more about God.

Looking back at my life and struggles in high school through personal reflection and through the talk I gave in grade twelve has been really beneficial in my life now. One of the main things I've reflected on is how so many of my struggles now, as an adult, compare to those I had in high school. The thing I struggle most with right now, similar to my struggles in grade ten, is trusting God and His plan. As I get older, I start to think more of my future, my career and my goals. I find myself asking God the same questions: "Why am I going through this?" or "What are your plans for my life?" I am always wondering why things aren't going the way I want it to, even when I seem to have everything planned out.

Going through the challenges in grade ten, and reading it back again, was a great reminder of how God moved, and continues to move, in my life. It reassures my belief in God because it shows how much He has done in my life. In grade ten, I thought my life was over! But because of the hardship, I was able to motivate myself to create a better life. Now, looking back on that, I am confident that the Lord has a reason for my struggles. Sometimes I still feel that pain I felt in grade ten, lost and alone, but now I know That God is present through my struggles and shaping me through them.

I remember in grade ten, when my two closest friends left and I was feeling lost and alone. I had no idea what to do. Going into university, I felt the exact same way. But this time was different because I knew that God helped me through it once, so He can do it again. It gave me another reason why I decided to remain Catholic.

Writing a talk in grade twelve and saying it in front of my peers has benefited and changed my life in many ways. In high school, it encouraged me to break from the busy student life and reflect on my life. In many ways, it helped me see the things I did and didn't like in my life, helping me improve through every situation. It also gave me so much courage and confidence to share my life to my peers. It was terrifying at times, but it made me feel more connected to my classmates because they were able to know who I really was.

Now, I find it so reassuring to read about my life and struggles because it is proof that I have survived them and it helps me learn from past mistakes. It shows me that God can use whatever happens to us for His own plan. As I keep reflecting on my story in high school, it gives me more clarity and meaning to so many questions I had. I always wondered why God would allow people to suffer or why I was always feeling lost. A simple answer is that life is not easy. But, something I have reflected on and learnt through Mr. Brock's response is that God is shedding us of our old lives to make our new life even better. He is making new wine.

To hear talks in high school also made me feel more connected to my classmates because it was a way for me to understand what they were going through and see the real them. In high school there are so many different types of people, and talks allowed us to get a deeper sense of what they go through day-to-day. The talks made me see life through the eyes of another student, who may or may not be going through the same thing as me.

It's been about three years since I left Saint Andrew's but I still find it impacting my life for the better every day. The retreats gave me the opportunity to delve deeper into my faith and helped me find time for myself amidst the craziness of school. Giving talks and hearing them provided so many opportunities to learn and reflect on my life. Being a retreat leader has helped me grow confident as a leader and in my identity as a daughter of God. The teachers believed in me in a way that inspired me to believe in myself. I was surrounded by so much love and I felt God's love through the students and staff. Because of this, I have felt a calling to become a teacher. My hope is to create that same environment that helped me grow in confidence and that helped me believe in myself. I am so inspired by the teachers and experiences I had and I hope that my students will also be able to find God in their lives.

If I could give my younger self any advice, or any teens in high school right now, it would be to not be afraid to ask questions or wonder about something. Don't hesitate to explore that one aspect of your life. Keep asking those hard questions because you won't get an answer if you don't ask. In grade ten I asked: "Where was God through my struggles?" Now I am asking Him: "What are you doing with my life?" and "What is my purpose?" By asking God those big questions and finding my personal relationship with God, the answers were revealed to me through the new life God has created for me. A life that I would have never known if I didn't ask those hard questions and go through those hard times. A key aspect that helped me realize and reflect on these questions was writing them down, in the form of doing a talk or even journaling. Take a moment to reflect on the hard questions you are asking. I know that God has many great answers and will show them to you throughout the journey of your life in the most unexpected ways.

4

Notes to a High School Retreat Director

"Each of us is a story. We were created by God as a
story waiting to be told, and each of us has to find a
way to tell our story."

—RICHARD ROHR, OFM

I teach religion and coordinate retreats in a Catholic high school,
and I have a problem. Am I working in the school or for the school?
Am I using the school to do my work, or am I doing the work of
the school? I will admit, I sometimes feel I am doing my own thing,
and sometimes I feel I'm doing the school's thing. It fluctuates, but
it shouldn't.

". . . Catholic schools proceed ex corde Ecclesiae, from the
very heart of the Church," writes Archbishop J. Michael Miller, CSB,
in a booklet entitled: *The Holy See's Teaching on Catholic Schools*.
Catholic schools, he continues, "must be integrated into the or-
ganic pastoral program of the parish, the diocese, and the universal
Church."[15]

I'm connected.

But sometimes it feels like the plug has fallen out of the socket.

The Catholic school is a ministry of the church, so we should all be working together, in communion, in the one body of Christ, building the Kingdom of God.

Yet, it seems, there are many fiefdoms in the one kingdom. Teachers have their own turf to defend and their own department's interest to promote. If you don't believe me, attend a staff meeting. This is not a weakness of the system, but a sign of vibrant life. Still, someone has to ensure that the life of the school is connected to the life of the church. The branch needs to stay connected to the vine. That someone is everyone, but mostly it is the principal. The principal is the pastoral minister of the school. It's not an easy job, which is why few want it.

The school is a conglomerate of sports, arts and academics. But wait a minute, where does religion fit in?

Jesus never spoke of religion as something that needs to "fit in." The Kingdom of God, Jesus said, is like a big net that gathers everybody. The Kingdom is like yeast that makes things rise. The Kingdom is like good seeds sown in a field that you can't distinguish from the weeds until harvest time. The Kingdom is like a tiny mustard seed, the least of all seeds, but when it grows becomes a tree for birds to nest.

The religious nature of the school is subtle, like yeast, but that is how it rises. It is hidden, like a seed, but that is where life is.

Presentation Brother J. Matthew Feheney edited *From Ideal to Action: The Inner Nature of a Catholic School Today*. Feheney contrasts the surface level with the deeper level (inner nature) of the Catholic school. He writes:

> The surface-level characteristics of a Catholic school that might catch the attention of a potential or actual parent or a member of the public might be: Success in public examinations, attractive uniform, success in sporting and other extracurricular activities, behavior of students in public, public relations image, and so on.
>
> At the deeper level however, the things that give a Catholic school its character are less obvious. They include: ethos, philosophy and mission statement of the school, approach to discipline, staff development, nature

of leadership, relationship between members of staff, religious education program, pastoral care program, and so on.

And then Feheney makes a salient point: "It is these inner characteristics that ultimately determine the nature of a Catholic school."[16]

There is the "surface characteristics" of our school and there is the "deeper level." Where do we put our emphasis? Where do we put our time, our talent and our treasure?

In our extraverted society, it is easier to polish our image than to attend to the "less obvious" things, like our spirit. And sometimes what is truly essential to our catholicity can be experienced as part of our image rather than being on "a deeper level," part of our character. We have to have Mass because we are a Catholic school, some say. But the reverse is more accurate: We are a Catholic school because we have Mass. The Mass is the sacrament of the real presence of Jesus. But if students do not experience the real presence of Jesus in the inner nature of the school, the real presence of Jesus in the Eucharist can elude them. The disciples on the road to Emmaus recognized Jesus in the breaking of the bread because they experienced him on the journey.

What do students feel, at an all school Mass, when informed by word and ritual that they are all "one body in Christ" when they know, by every day experience, that his or her grade is divided into groups who don't acknowledge each other, who rank each other, who stereotype each other and who covertly, and sometimes overtly, conflict with each other. What do students feel? They feel nothing.

Is our Catholic school driven by outer characteristics that we then try to "fit" religion into? Is religion just another department jockeying for influence?

We need outward signs of our Catholicity. We need Masses in the calendar, crucifixes on the wall and doctrine in religion class. But something else is needed to help our students see what these signs signify.

This something is like Jesus's net that gathers everybody. It is the yeast that lifts kids' spirits. It is the seed that grows into a school where kids can nest. It is what Feheney calls the "less obvious" things.

I have come to see that this something is essential to forming the "inner nature" of a Catholic school. This something is necessary to ensure that the life of the school is connected to the life of the church. This something is student-led retreats.

So crucial are student-led retreats to the catholicity of the school that I believe they should be enshrined in the mission statement of the school.

There are two reasons for this:

1. Student-led retreats are necessary to build a community of compassion among our students.
2. Student-led retreats must be protected because they are an endangered species and risk extinction.

1. STUDENT-LED RETREATS ARE NECESSARY.

Question: How do you turn this . . .

> *My class always feels so divided, I am scared to be who I am because of how judgmental everyone is. I feel so unimportant. . . . In my opinion, my class keeps going down hill.*

> *We've really grown apart and I honestly think we've made a lot of bad choices. We've separated into cliques and pretty much nobody hangs out with any clique other than their "own." I also feel like everybody is a lot more judgmental and not as accepting as we used to be.*

> *Sometimes people are excluded and no one seems to do anything about it, so it just gets brushed off.*

> *My class believes in social hierarchy.*

> *I feel like there's the popular people and I'm just the background music to their story.*

Rifts and cracks are forming in our class.

Help, we need some fun!

Into this . . .

Yes, oh my goodness, yes. I really got to see the true grade 10 class and it was cool. I can't believe that it was our class at Camp Imadene.

I feel that I can be with anyone now and just hang out with them. Thank you sooo much. Such a good time and a wonderful experience.

Barriers have been broken down, and so many friendships have been formed. Thank you for making this one of the best experiences of my whole school career. This retreat is something I will never forget.

It brought us together. It really has. We were very far from each other by November. We hung on only by a thread. We needed this retreat to bring us closer to each other. And that is exactly what it did.

This retreat has helped me to really grow in my faith. I originally planned not to go, because I am not Catholic and I was worried about every small detail. I'm so glad I decided to go in the end, because this is something I'm going to remember for the rest of my life. I really felt the love within the class on this retreat. This retreat has made me optimistic about the future of humanity.

For the first time ever I wasn't nervous to go to school today.

Answer: Student-led retreats. One student wrote on the pre-retreat anonymous evaluation form:

We all have something to contribute to the grade, we just need an environment to accommodate it.

The "environment to accommodate it" is the student-led retreat.

The "something" that kids have to contribute to the grade is themselves. The gift of themselves that kids give each other is the gift of their vulnerability, and vulnerability is the only way a community of compassion can be formed.

Vulnerability is not a "tell-all"; it is not "seeking attention"; it is not being "totally open" or "spilling the beans." Vulnerability is not "all-about-me." I am indebted to Mark W. Baker who taught me what vulnerability is:

> Vulnerability is taking the risk to expose yourself emotionally. You will feel very uncertain while doing it, but there is no other path to the most meaningful experiences you will ever have. We were created for the purpose of connection to God and others, and vulnerability is the requirement for achieving that purpose . . .
>
> It is actually through our painful emotional experiences that we learn life's greatest lessons. Our greatest insights, most intimate connections with others, and the development of our most crucial capacities to deal with life come in the emotional valleys, not during our mountaintop experiences.[17]

Popular usage of the word vulnerable means weakness. We may say, for instance, that the very old are vulnerable, or those with learning difficulties or those with compromised immune systems. Here, vulnerability is understood as a lack of strength.

The vulnerability of students who tell their stories on retreat is not the vulnerability of revealed weakness, but the vulnerability of revealed needs. It is not weakness to need love, to need worth, to need belonging, to need acceptance, to need joy. It is not a weakness to have painful feelings. But revealing your needs and feelings, and owning them without blame or criticism of others is a way of revealing yourself that is "vulnerable" to being hurt by other people's criticism or rejection. *Yet, it is the only way to build a culture of compassion in the school.*

This is the vulnerability of little children who express their needs openly. This is the vulnerability of Jesus who cried over Jerusalem, who revealed his sorrowful soul in the upper room, who called for his friends at Gethsemane, who cried out "I thirst" from the cross and who asked Peter on the shores of Lake Galilee, "Do you love me?" Jesus is the vulnerability of God.

When we lose faith that God is present in our life—all of our life—then we lose the idea that being vulnerable is a prayerful and sacred experience. When we lose faith, strength is understood as power over others, rather than power over our own fear of being ourself. Then, egocentricity reigns, and the kingdom of domination over others becomes the playbook. We see this in history. We see this in our own times with authoritarian governments on the rise. I saw it in my classroom the other day when a student, a girl, revealed in class discussion that it seems in present day culture that tenderness—being tender, is viewed as a sign of weakness.

Vulnerability is not weakness, but strength—the courage to be who we are. And vulnerability is the only way we connect to our true self, to God and to others, which is the purpose for which we were created.

> *The retreat helped me open up the feelings that I wanted to keep buried inside. I let myself be vulnerable and it helped me find a part of myself.*

> *I let myself be vulnerable and it helped me. Vulnerability takes courage.*

On retreats, with the help of student leaders, students let themselves be vulnerable. When this happens they have their greatest insights (faith), most intimate connections (love) and develop a capacity to deal with life (hope).

A student-led retreat, by definition, is a team of grade eleven and twelve students, who meet for two hours, once a week, for six weeks, to prepare a retreat for students in the lower grades (grade eight, nine and ten). These meetings are formation meetings, not just information meetings.

On a student-led retreat, an adult directs, but students lead. Whereas I direct by overseeing the retreat schedule and by interjecting where needed, students lead by giving talks, facilitating small group discussions, performing skits and taking initiative in icebreakers and games. Students lead, mostly, by example. They "prime-the-pump" of retreatant enthusiasm and communicate by their presence that this is a "youth-friendly event."

Student leaders are older mentors that younger students look up to (except on the grade twelve retreat, where grade twelve student leaders serve their own class). When student leaders give talks, the retreatants' attention merits the use of the expression that measures the level of quiet by being able to "hear a pin drop." Student leaders also serve the director as guides and interpreters of adolescent culture.

Every event and activity on the retreat is purposed and planned, like the colors on a canvas or notes in a musical composition. A retreat is an artwork. Sequence and timing are intentional.

Take play. We play on retreat. We call them icebreakers. What is the goal of play? The goal of play is play itself.

In traditional cultures, play, like dance, was esteemed as sacred ritual. I know this. I look back to my childhood play as a secret garden, a lost paradise. In play I was in the moment, engaged, unselfconscious, alive in all my senses and connected to others. Play is a child's contemplation.

We play on retreats. We play Fruit Basket, People Bingo, The Bear Family, Pictionary, Shuffle Your Buns, Human Knot, Hoola Hoop Pass, Birdie on the Perch, Clumps and, of course, Capture the Flag.

Experienced youth ministers and retreat directors know which games to play, when, and with what age level.

> *The icebreakers are my favorite!!! All the games were fun and great.*
>
> *These games strengthened the bonds of our class in such a fun way.*
>
> *After playing this game I made a lot of new friends.*
>
> *It was great to see everyone come out and enjoy each other's company.*
>
> *Very fun. Ice-breakers are the best, honestly—love them.*

Fun, play, skits, talks, discussions, prayer, communal meals, dance, reconciliation, eucharist—these are the elements of the art of student-led retreats.

At the retreat team formation meetings (14–16 students) we do what we want the younger students to do on retreat. We practice what we will preach. We form bonds. We do skits. We play together and we pray together. And we practice our "talks"—not a speech, not a lecture, not a dissertation on a topic, not an exhortation on an issue—just a talk. The talk is a gift from a student leader to the retreatants to help them on their life journey. It is an act of love. It is the student leaders' story. So essential are student talks, that I would describe such a retreat as: student-led/student-talk retreat.

A student-led/student-talk retreat can be contrasted with a theme-based retreat. In a theme-based retreat, a theme (topic) is chosen from religious beliefs/teachings, and the retreat program serves that topic.

A theme based retreat is easier to organize. An adult driven planning group brainstorming religious activities for teens in the hope that something will stick. This is an outside-trying-to-get-in-retreat, rather than an inside-trying-to-get-out-retreat. In a student-led/student-talk retreat, the students' own stories are at the heart of the retreat and the retreat program proceeds from that heart.

My contention is that a student-led/student-talk retreat best serves the needs of students, and makes a beneficial and enduring difference in their lives and in the life of the school. I find that students try to use a theme-based retreat to meet their needs creating two retreats: the retreat the students are trying to have, and the retreat the adults have planned. A student-led/student-talk retreat unites these two by working with the needs and desires of youth, where, I believe, God is present in their life.

A talk has four steps:

1. Introduction of self
2. My story
3. I learned
4. I challenge you

Talks are between 8–10 minutes, but the bulk of the talk is the "My story" part. The "My story" part is the vulnerability part, as students share their personal experiences and the lessons they have learned. My job as retreat director is to help students find their voice without putting words in their mouth.

I once took students to a youth conference of over seven hundred youth. The conference featured a teen who gave a talk. At the end of the talk, one of my students turned to me and said, "She didn't write that. Her mother wrote that. Some adult wrote that. Kids don't say those things. Kids don't talk like that. No way!"

Kids know. When kids talk like adults, adults say, "Isn't that nice." But other kids say, "That's not real."

One student leader, who was considering giving a talk, said to me, "I just want to make sure that my talk helps the students. That is the reason I'm willing to give the talk." This is why they meet with me first. We discern together, and ensure that the speaker is willing, the story is prudent, the lesson is relatable and the challenge is consistent with Gospel values.

It is not easy being vulnerable in front of your peers and younger students, but student leaders are willing to be vulnerable "If it helps the students." It does help them. It evokes compassion within them and builds community among them.

> The retreat helped me realize that I need to be more empathetic and compassionate and less judgmental.

> What I gained from this retreat was to always be kind to your classmates.

> I recognize, in a better way, that everyone experiences hardships and tribulations and I believe this will affect the way I treat others for the rest of my life.

"Compassion," according to religious scholar, Karen Armstrong, "does not mean feeling sorry for people, or feeling pity for them. It means feeling *with* someone else. That's what the Golden Rule says. Look into your own heart, find out what gives you pain, and refuse to inflict that pain on anyone else . . . and not just your group, but everybody."[18]

Students give their talk to me, the retreat director—one person. Then they give their talk to the retreat team—fourteen people. Then they give their talk to the class on retreat—seventy people.

For most, it is the first time they have told their story to anyone. It is difficult to go back to the land of painful feelings. Painful feelings in teens, particularly in our present cultural milieux, translates as there-is-something-wrong-with-me. Giving a talk is an opportunity to go back to those feelings and treat them with compassion, rather than shame. Giving their talk first to me, then to the retreat team, is not just a practice, it is a healing.

> But, in telling Barbara my story, I had felt a great lifting of the spirit, a cleansing and scouring and airy rising of the soul toward light. I felt what truth tasted like, and it rolled like honey off my tongue.[19]
> Pat Conroy

Being compassionate toward yourself requires a different way of seeing and understanding your emotions—painful and pleasurable. This involves understanding the value of feelings as a gateway to knowledge and understanding. "Feelings," notes the website of BioSpirituality, "are like the phone ringing, a message is trying to get through."[20]

I help students explore what that message may be. This helps with the "I learned" and "I challenge you" part of their talk.

When student leaders share their story, and the emotions they feel while sharing it, they communicate to the class sitting before them: It's ok to acknowledge your emotions, it's ok to go through tough times, it's good to treat yourself and others with compassion.

Student talks help the student giving the talk and they help the students who hear the talk. Student talks help. Here are four ways.

1. Removing Barriers

The talks help students to remove the barriers between them and God. Many students hide a pain-filled part of their heart. They are alone with their pain. They fear it makes them less of a person. They feel unworthy. The door of their heart is shut—even to God. But

God, in Jesus, has descended into our pain, and has come to liberate us. The talks show the students that they are not alone in their pain and gives them the courage to open the door.

> They talked about a lot of problems that I am struggling with, so it was very helpful.

> I understood why it was good to open up.

> I honestly didn't know that all of them had some really hard times like me.

2. God In The "Now"

The talks help students see that God comes to them just as they are. For many students, God is "something" outside themselves that adults are trying to get them to buy into. They see religion as something promoting an ideal version of yourself in the future, remote and possibly unattainable. The talks show that God comes to us in the "now," in our life. Students don't see their ordinary life as meaningful, revelatory, or worth reflecting on. The talks change that.

> The student leadership talks brought light to many situations that aren't usually talked about.

> I thought the talks were amazing. They all moved me deeply and forced me to reflect on myself and my actions. I really think I changed a bit from the talks.

3. Binding Us Together

"It is impossible to overemphasize," wrote Dr. Paul Tournier, "the immense need humans have to be really listened to, to be taken seriously, to be understood."[21]

A student giving a talk thinks: There is a part of me I want others to understand. For this to happen I need to tell my story. I am not sure how others will respond, but I will take the risk.

When they do, the listening students think: Me, too.

Connection.

Bonding.

I've seen this happen on every retreat. The student leaders lead by example, and the class follows.

> *The talks helped me get a deeper understanding of my classmates and made me realize that I didn't know them as well as I thought I did.*

> *The students that gave the talks have definitely brought our grade closer and stronger, resulting in a better "family."*

4. Where Love Is, There Is God

The talks inspire students to love God, love others and love self.

> *I felt the talks were amazing! Being able to express how you feel and also because people are actually listening to you and understanding you.*

> *After this retreat I feel loved and I talk to so many people I usually don't talk to.*

> *The student leadership talks put something in my heart.*

On retreats we don't give kids God. We give them an opportunity to take down the barriers inside themselves and find God who is already, and has always been, with them.

> *At first when I came to this school I didn't know what I believed in. I thought there was something out there, but I didn't know how to find it. This retreat made me believe in God.*

Listening to kids' real life stories is the theme of Patricia Hersh's celebrated work, *A Tribe Apart*, written over twenty years ago. Kids are a tribe apart but they don't want to be. They want to be known and they want a dependable and committed relationship with a supportive adult. At the end of the book Hersh tells the story of a girl who shares herself and her song with her peers who are gathered before her in a large auditorium. She is a girl who thought of taking her life more than once. In the middle of the song she is overcome with tears. Her class "wraps its arms around her with applause." She was afraid people would "take my feelings and just reject them." But the opposite happened. She says, "Tonight was the best spiritual experience I've ever had."[22]

Connection.

I know this "spiritual experience." I see it on every retreat. This experience should not be an exceptional luxury in our school. It should be standard fare, "part-of-the-curriculum." We preach church to kids but we won't let them be church. If we don't provide for such experiences we are not allowing our youth to be the young church today. But that is the only church they can authentically and uniquely be. That is the church they do best.

Instead, we are content if they read or write Mass intentions or serve at the altar or bring up the gifts. All good service youth can do. But adults can do this as well. What can teens give that no one else can? How can they be not the "church of the future," but the young church of today? One thing they can do, that no one else can, is tell their story.

> I think it was really cool how these people were brave enough to say their stories.

> I loved the openness and the honesty. . . . I will remember these talks for the rest of my life.

> Whenever I see the student retreat leaders in the halls, I look at them differently, but in a good way. And I remember, everyone has a story.

> I have gained so much from this retreat. I was incredibly inspired by the leaders' stories and I was touched by their willingness to share something so personal with us. It was amazing.

Dang! Those were deep words coming from sixteen and seventeen year olds.

The bottom line is this, says the author of *A Tribe Apart*: ". . . we can lecture kids to our hearts' content but if they don't care what we think, or there is no relationship between us that matters to them, or they think we are ignorant of the reality of their lives, they will not listen."[23]

Students need to tell their story, but they need an adult to help them. They need an adult to encourage them and guide them. They need encouragement to believe that what they have to say is worth saying. They need guidance to help them find their own voice to say it. They need help remembering the details, for the power of a story is always in the details. I have sat down with hundreds of students and helped them write their stories. Helping students write their stories and then receiving that story on the retreat has been the greatest blessing I have received in my work with youth. This is what stirs my soul and transports me to a place where I see God. Student talks have evangelized me. During a talk I begin to see that student's soul; I get glimpses of their heart. It is a new way of seeing for me. It is the way Jesus always sees. I physically feel numb after a talk. I feel weak. My eyes sometimes water, my heart always softens. After a retreat kids say they have to go back to the "real world." But this is the real world, everything else seems fake. Dear God, help me not forget that kid's talk, how I felt hearing it and what it has done to me. Take away my heart of stone and give me a heart of flesh.

In Luke 24:13, Jesus encounters two forlorn strangers on the Emmaus road. "What are you discussing with each other as you walk along?," asks Jesus. What is your story? They tell. Jesus listens and explains to them the significance of their story. Your story reveals the paschal mystery of death and rebirth. Your story reflects the biblical story. There is meaning here. God is in your story.

"Were not our hearts burning," the travelers say to each other. "Come, stay with us," they say to Jesus whom they only recognize later in the sacred ritual of the Eucharist. This is what happens on retreats, when, after all the student talks, we recognize God in the sacrament of Reconciliation and Eucharist. Then, as the travelers did in the Emmaus story, we can turn around, and go back to our life with renewed hope.

Just to know others have experienced this too.

Just to know I am not alone.

Just to know this is a normal problem.

Just to know you can talk about it.

Just to know you can have problems, but there is hope.

Just to know that others have been there, have survived, and therefore, so can I.

Just to know.

The entire retreat, which is an experience of spiritual immersion, builds a culture of compassion, and the talks are at the heart of the process. After each talk, the students meet in small groups to share their response to the talk. This is their chance to "open up," to be vulnerable themselves. They can do this because there is acceptance and love in the room. The student leaders have led by example. Their message is clear: Be strong enough to admit your weakness and be open enough to receive the love you need.

> *The small group discussions were just very awkward at first . . . but then it started to mean something, we weren't afraid to voice how we felt and that slowly brought everyone together.*

> *It took some time to open up and actually say what we think rather than what we think we should say.*

Any given grade level, in any given school, at any given time, is either getting better or getting bitter. No class is standing still. The grade will be moving toward the kingdom of domination or the kingdom of compassion; the kingdom of coolness or the kingdom of love. We all know what the kingdom of domination and coolness looks like. It's almost what we expect.

> *A part of our class acts like they are better than everyone else. They are obsessed with social media.*

> *They make fun of people because they are different, they judge a lot.*

People talk to you or they ignore you . . . people don't welcome others. They have their cliques and that's final.

People are ditching their friends to hang out with people who will make them popular.

There is the judging mafia that every grade has. There are a lot of cliques which really bugs me. I would give anything for us to be just one big group.

There is a void between 'popular/athletic/media people' and 'uncool' people. Maybe one day we can all be friends, but right now, that is nothing but a dream.

At the end of the day I don't feel that I belong.

The kingdom of compassion looks like this:

I dropped all resentment toward some classmates.

The groups that are so defined in the hallways were gone. The barriers of our clique groups were broken and we could bond without judgements of talking to people outside your comfort zone.

I love this school more than ever. I am so very happy to be here and I don't want to miss a moment. It fully restored my spirit and love for school.

I thought being friends with students I don't know was hard. . . . However, this retreat helped me connect.

It helped me understand that popularity wasn't something you need to get through high school and that being myself wasn't anything to be afraid of.

It has brought our whole grade together. I think if I was in a different school, we would not have these opportunities to come together and talk. Thank you. It is a rare opportunity and a really great one.

I learned that nobody has a perfect life, we all have our struggles no matter how perfect they may seem on the surface. It just made me want to give everyone a hug!

In every school, it seems, there are the cool and uncool, the popular and unpopular, the ones who gather in groups, laugh and make noise, and those who don't. There is a "them" and "us," or a "them" and "no bodies." There are kids walking the hallways with the conviction that they are inferior to others and that if anyone really knew them, they would be even more rejected. And then there are the kids who seem to have it all together—smart, talented, good looking, popular, near perfect lives. But the truth is, they are also wounded. Walking the hallways trying to keep their image intact, trying not to show weakness, trying not to be too serious—it takes a lot of energy to hide the truth of one's self. Can this truth be revealed? How can it be when it is locked up so tight!

It is revealed on retreats. It is revealed in the talks and small group sharings. It is revealed because kids want others to know the "real me."

This retreat helped me by teaching me I don't need to pretend to be someone to impress others.

Before I felt I needed to be amazing at everything to be popular. Now, I just need to be myself.

I have more confidence in myself knowing everyone in my class wants the same love and acceptance that I do.

The beauty isn't in our perfection, it's in our struggles.

This was probably the only time I felt like I wasn't invisible to 95% of the people in my grade.

I am so thankful for the community here at our high school. When I come to school, I feel worried, but that feeling goes away because I know there is someone I can talk to and not judge me. School feels like a second home. It's where I can laugh, cry and make memories matter.

Until and unless this happens in high school, we bear the name Catholic as more of a brand or logo, rather than a dynamic reality. Until and unless this happens in high school, the Kingdom of God will diminish and the kingdom of coolness will reign. This will happen not because the kids at the top of the social hierarchy are bad, or mean, or bullies, but because they are "smart" enough to discern the ways-of-the-world and they have learned how the game works.

But the kids at the "top" want liberation as much as the kids at the "bottom." They want to be loved for who they are and not the mask they wear and the role they play. They, too, want the Kingdom Jesus inaugurated and was passionate about. The Kingdom of God can break out anywhere in the school, but I see the Kingdom happening in a powerful way on retreats. It happens on retreats because that is the intentional plan and purpose of retreats. It is not a matter of chance, but purpose and planning and preparing. It takes time and it takes work. Retreat planning is more perspiration than inspiration. But when it is done and done right, the school is a different school because of it.

> I was thinking of switching schools, like seriously considering it. After this retreat I now know for a fact that I am staying at St. Andrew's. The people are amazing. I got so much closer with my classmates and I truly had an amazing time.

> I think the retreat brought our entire class close together and made us realize that the school really does care about us whether we believe it or not.

> Words can't explain how thankful I am for experiencing this retreat. . . . Probably the best three days of my high school career . . . maybe even in life.

> It saddens me that no other school goes on retreats like this, because it makes such a huge positive impact on everyone. The world would be a much better place if everyone got the chance to go on retreats. I'm so glad retreats are a part of our school.

This retreat is fixing wounds that have hurt for four years.

I found God in my school.

Thank you. The retreats are always something I look forward to. I know they are a ton of work and I truly appreciate them.

When I say organizing and facilitating a retreat is hard work, I do not mean that the divine gift, grace, is bought for a price. God's grace is free, not earned and not manipulated. After six weeks of retreat preparation (hard work) I say a little prayer on the bus on the way to the retreat destination. It is a prayer of letting go, and letting God. I thank God for allowing me to be a part of this ministry, and then "I" get out of the way. On the second night of the retreat you can see it. "Someone" has taken charge, and it's not me. Still, I have a joke with God: Why do I have to do all the "bull work?" The answer is in the Scriptures: Blessed are the humble for they shall be exhausted (I think it says that).

We don't go on retreat to find ourselves. We go on retreat to find one another. In doing so we find ourselves. Again, Mark W. Baker: "Psychologists no longer talk about humans having an individual self, we talk about having a sense of self in the context of our relationships. For you to be you, you need God and others."[24]

This has changed how I teach "Identity"—the task of adolescence. I used to see identity as an idea about yourself that you only discover by looking within yourself. This is akin to the prevalent cultural concept of individualism. I now understand our identity as not an idea of self but "a sense of self," and not from just searching within oneself but "in the context of our relationships." The doctrine of the Trinity teaches us that God is a relationship, oneness in three. If we are created in the image and likeness of God, then, who we are is, like God, a person in relationship. And, if this is at the core of our faith, then helping to build loving relationships among the student body is our primary task in the Catholic high school. And if "vulnerability is the requirement for achieving this purpose" then retreats should be at the very heart of the mission of the school.

If we don't have student-led retreats are we not like those of whom Jesus spoke: They tie up heavy burdens, hard to bear, and lay them on the shoulders of others; but they themselves are unwilling to lift a finger to move them (Matthew 23:4). Isn't that what we do when we teach teens religion in the classroom but don't give them the help they need to practice it in the hallways? The help they need is a student-led retreat. Otherwise religious education is like giving kids a menu, but not letting them eat.

Students, too, can find themselves in the same dilemma I found myself as stated at the beginning of this chapter. Am I using the school to get a diploma, or am I part of the school community? Am I here for my own purpose, or do I share in, and contribute to, the purpose of the school?

"A spirituality of communion," writes Archbishop J. Michael Miller, "should be the guiding principle of Catholic education. Without this spiritual path, all external structures of cooperation serve very little purpose; they would be mere mechanisms without a soul."[25]

Catholic schools must care for the souls of our students. Otherwise we grind along as "mere mechanisms," propping up our "outer characteristics" and forgetting who we are. At the conclusions of his book, Archbishop Miller calls for a "collaborative and systematic exercise of assessing a school's catholicity" in order to, "identify, clarify and strengthen its effectiveness in its service of Christ and the Church."[26] I would like to suggest anonymous pre-and-post retreat evaluation forms as an essential component of this assessment.

2. STUDENT-LED RETREATS ARE ENDANGERED.

"Mr. Brock, I can't be a retreat leader because I can't make the meetings. I have hockey practice."

"Mr. Brock, I can't join the team, I have ballet every day after school."

"Mr. Brock, I can't join the retreat team, I'm taking an Advanced Placement Course (AP) and I'm too stressed out and I have to study. I have no time."

"Mr. Brock, my volleyball coach says I have to be at practice, so if I join the retreat team, I have to leave the meetings half way through."

"Mr. Brock, I work after school and my boss won't let me take the time off."

"Mr. Brock . . . (fill in the blank)"

The "trickle down theory" may not work economically, but it works in this case. All the stress, busyness and mental health challenges of adulthood have trickled down to youth. They don't have time to be young. They don't have time to be.

Only five years ago, when I put out a call for 14–16 student leaders for an upcoming retreat, I would receive 20, 25, sometimes 35 application forms. My biggest problem was saying "no" to some students. I hated that task. I'd write a letter affirming their gifts and talents while explaining why I "couldn't get you on the team this time." No matter, they always saw it as a rejection letter.

I'm glad I don't have to send that letter out anymore. But I have a new problem. Over the last few years only 5, 6 or 7 students apply. Everyone else is "too busy." Everyone else has a coach or boss who owns them. Everyone else is stressed out with school. Everyone else is busy on their cell phone!

I beat a path in the hallways looking for recruits. After meeting 6 or 7 times as a retreat leadership team students say to me, "I'm going to miss these retreat meetings." That's because at meetings we turn stressed into blessed.

We meet in the parish hall up the hill from school. That's so we can separate ourselves from bells and announcements and the work-aura of school. We find sacred space to Be still, and know that I am God! (Psalm 46:10).

Student-led retreats are endangered and the problem is not just with students, but with adults. No student should say to themselves: Well, I'd like to be a retreat leader, but my coach won't like that. No student should fear that their position on a sports team becomes jeopardized because they want to be a retreat leader. No student should have to choose between sports and arts and academics and being a retreat leader. It is a sad day in a Catholic school when our academic scholars, our sports champions and our theatre and musical stars are too busy to help our younger students as retreat leaders. A student should see a clear path to being a retreat leader and that path must be cleared by the principal of the school, the guardian of the vision of the school and the protector of the catholicity of the school. Retreat leadership teams and school retreats must not be seen as just another activity in the school equal to every other activity in the school. Retreat leadership teams and school retreats must be given special protection, distinct status, and preferential treatment. Like an old growth forest it must be protected or we will lose it.

This is not to say that retreats are important and athletics, arts and academics are not as important. This is not to say that retreats are sacred and athletics, arts and academics are not sacred. This is to say that retreats are like the Sabbath day in relation to every other day. Remember, says the Decalogue, to keep the Sabbath day holy. Every day is the Lord's day, just like every year (anno domine) is the Lord's year. So when Jews set apart Saturday; Christians, Sunday; and Muslims, Friday, it is not because one day of the week is more holy than the others, but because we can lose the sense of the holiness of all days if we don't protect this one day.

My contention is this: Retreats are the Sabbath day of the school. What the retreat program creates, in a significant way, is a culture of compassion in the school. Everything in the school is sacred. But without student-led retreats we lose the sacredness of athletics, arts and academics. Without student-led retreats, social hierarchy forms. Then the Kingdom of domination gets a foothold. Then it becomes all about me, not we. Then it divides the school into us and them, into winners and losers, into cool and uncool. Then we pride the school exclusively on "success in public examinations . . . success in sporting and other extracurricular activities," rather than the inner nature of the school which is a culture of compassion. When this happens the mechanism of the school continues, but it has lost its soul.

Retreats are places where we see teenagers and where we see the Kingdom of God—two terms usually not associated together.

I'm a happier person now. I'm not angry or sad all the time. I also love my grad class and I feel loved which I have never felt in such capacity.

When everyone hugged and forgave each other, I had never felt more love and connection in a community before in my life.

I have matured and, I believe, grown way closer to God. I am fully at peace with life because God has healed everything and I know I have a great future in simply following Him.

I cannot stress how much this retreat helped me. I've been smiling ever since. I now have the motivation to be myself and talk to new people. So many people said nice things about me and it felt amazing.
I am so thankful for this retreat as I learned to be more positive about myself and my situation.

Thank you for getting us together on all our retreats throughout the years. They are my favorite memories of high school.

I hope retreats never end.

Dear friends, celebrating the Sacrament of Reconciliation means being enfolded in a warm embrace; it is the embrace of the Father's infinite mercy.[27]
Pope Francis

I was once asked to direct a diocesan youth retreat. On the final evening I planned, as I do on school retreats, the Sacrament of Reconciliation. A few priests, as well as the bishop arrived. At the end of the evening the bishop came to me and said, "I like what you did. We didn't have just Reconciliation available, we had a Reconciliation service."

Previously, in past diocesan retreats, the director announced a set time for Reconciliation, and informed the youth where the priests were stationed—down a hallway to the left and in a room behind the stage. That space was off limits to everyone else, and was available for those who wished to receive the Sacrament.

My plan was to have all the youth stay in one big meeting room, with the priests as well, in a space cordoned off for privacy. Introduction, lights low, candles lit, reflective music, examination of conscience, priests ready, everyone together—that's what our bishop meant by "reconciliation service." The reason the bishop liked it, is because he saw what happened. No pressure was exerted on the youth, but, being together, they supported each other. They supported each other by example and by encouragement. That's how Reconciliation works for youth. Private confession in a supportive communal setting.

After private confession is complete there is something else that happens in our reconciliation service. I encourage students to mingle with their peers and ask forgiveness and offer some sign of reconciliation to anyone they have ignored or hurt in any way so that when we leave the room we are in right-relationship with everyone. That's what happens and it looks like a celebration, because it is. They are ready to do this because they have experienced God's mercy and compassion in the Sacrament of Reconciliation and because they have been immersed in a culture of compassion since the retreat began. Their hearts have been softened and they are ready to reach out to others. This is the reconciliation service our bishop liked and the students love. It is also what every grade in every school needs.

> I'm glad we have reconciliation on these retreats. I would hardly go to confession on my own, but it's always so good on retreats. All your friends are there to support you after you are done. It's just a super friendly and very safe environment.

> Reconciliation was a great way to connect with God, but as well with the people around you. I found everyone was super open and vulnerable towards each other.

No matter if you are religious or not, reconciliation would always help you. The priests were wise and they gave me really helpful advice.

Although I am not Catholic, I still felt how holy it was. That was awesome.

Nervous at first, but the priests were super kind and made me feel comfortable. I knew there would be no judgement and I'm glad I was given that opportunity.

Well I know everyone was tearing up, including me.

The retreat removed our "high-school-y" perspective of each other and shifted it to see each other as actual people.

God always feels present when we do reconciliation.

Reconciliation is the best part of the retreat. Having Bishop Gary there was so nice and all the priests were so welcoming. It truly was such a relief and compassion filled experience.

I noticed a change in Karen the way you notice things but don't take note. Then her mom met me in the parking lot and said, "Thanks for the retreat, Karen's changed."

It was a bona fide durable change, the weight-off-my-back change that put a little light and a freshly minted smile on Karen's face. And it withstood the test of time—the retreat was months ago. "She's changed," her mother said again, "She's happier."

"What did it?" I asked.

"Don't know," she said. "Karen mentioned the talks . . . just the whole retreat. When she came home she cried for days, but it was a sunshower cry, really . . . she's changed."

Karen cried for herself, the self she hid from others for so long. She cried for the self she didn't like because it wasn't as good as everyone else's self. She cried because she had rejected the little frightened girl she was. Karen could only see the bad space she was in when she got in a good space on retreat. When she saw it, she cried, and she cried for joy.

Before the retreat, Karen hovered in the background. Now Karen is ready to find her place in the world. Before the retreat you could say Karen was depressed. You could say she had social anxiety. You could say she had low self esteem, or chronic stress, or . . . you could say she's in grade ten. She's sixteen. She's not a problem to be fixed, she's an adolescent becoming.

That kids go through a hard time in adolescence is not the problem. It is the beginning of a life changing solution. But they need some help to guide them through it.

Much of the pain kids go through are spiritual growing pains. But they follow societal prompts and call it a "mental health problem" or "mental illness." But it is not an illness if your soul is asserting itself and trying to secure its rightful place as the engine of your life which has been usurped by subservience to external culture's fads and trends and the "strange gods" of social media.

This is not to diminish, in any way, the depth of pain youth experience when they go through hard times. Often, when they are hurting, they suffer alone, for they neither have the words to describe it or the wherewithal to talk about it. When they come to me, their pain has subsided, but their tears show how the painful memory is still etched in their heart. They can only see the time when they fell apart, but I see a time when they were building up—a new wine skin for new wine. Mostly it is the same overarching story, the paschal mystery: Christ has died, Christ has risen, Christ will come again.

What happened to Karen on retreat is the hope that author and therapist Larry Crabb, expressed in his book, *Connecting*: "I am now working toward the day when communities of God's people, ordinary Christians whose lives regularly intersect, will accomplish most of the good that we now depend on mental health professionals to provide. And they will do it by *connecting* with each other in ways that only the gospel makes possible."[28]

I'm happy for Karen and her mom. There is a light in Karen's eyes now, a light that used to be under a basket. Sometimes kids need to see an adult professional to help them. Sometimes they just need other teens on retreat.

In the middle of a retreat, years ago, a student asked me the following: "A friend of mine from the public school is passing by this way and I was wondering if he can stop by the retreat for a little while?"

I ordinarily would say, "no." Retreats are not drop-in centers and those who attend should be prepared for what they are attending. But I knew this girl and I trusted her discernment and I said, "yes."

The boy arrived, participated in an ice breaker, heard a couple of student talks, contributed to a small group discussion, and then had to leave. Before he left, he made this announcement to our students: "We could never do this in our school."

His words sounded like an emphatic statement. But I heard a hint of a question and a plea: Do you think we could do this in our school?

The picture of this student, standing there, making his statement and then departing, stays with me. At the time I said nothing, only waved goodbye.

I will say now to the reader what I wish I had said to that boy.

Yes we can!

Yes we must!

5

Notes to a High School Religion Teacher

"Unless we are comfortable inhabiting and spending
time in our own inner selves, it will be impossible
to share this with our students. And if we haven't
mastered this second language of conversation
with God, which is prayer, our teaching as Catholic
educators will be empty."[29]

—FATHER JAMES MULLIGAN, CSC

Teaching religion is the hardest subject in high school. The reason
is your subject is your students. Every other subject teaches a body
of knowledge: a body of math, a body of science, a body of history.
You don't teach a body of knowledge, you teach a somebody.

You may ask: What about theology, that's a body of knowledge, isn't it?

Your students are children of God and bear the image of God
within them. You are teaching them to be who they are, and you are
using theology to do so. Theology, the study of God, is really the
study of who we are in God's eye. Theology is not for God, it is for
us. This is why the bishops of the United States call high school religious education a "comprehensive program of pastoral ministry."

The most effective catechetical programs for adolescents
are integrated into a comprehensive program of pastoral
ministry for youth that includes catechesis, community
life, evangelization, justice and service, leadership development, pastoral care, and prayer and worship.[30]
National Directory for Catechesis

Yes, high school religious education "includes catechesis"
(theology) but only in the context of a comprehensive ministry to
youth. In this ministry theology becomes "applied theology," that is,
caring for the soul of the adolescent.

Bishop Robert Barron, in his illuminating Foreword to the
2003 edition of *The Great Mysteries* by Father Andrew Greeley,
writes: "The Catholic theologian Hans Urs von Balthasar said that
the greatest tragedy in the history of Christianity was . . . the split
that opened up between theology and spirituality at the end of the
Middle Ages." "In the early centuries of the Church's life," Bishop
Barron continues, "the most influential theologians were not academics in our sense of the term . . . they wrote . . . to doctor souls."[31]

This split between theology and spirituality produced a "dryly
propositional and uninspiring catechesis." High school religious
education should reconnect theology and spirituality so as to doctor the souls of teenagers, what I understand as "pastoral ministry."
Pastoral ministry, on retreat and in the classroom, is what builds a
culture of compassion in the Catholic high school.

Maybe there was a time in the past when community life,
evangelization, justice and service, leadership development, pastoral
care and prayer and worship already took place in the lives of youth.
A time when the Catholic neighborhood took care of the Catholic
teenager. A time when the parish was the prominent pedagogy because it was the social hub. All religious educators had to do was
pose theological questions and answer them. All we needed for catechesis was a catechism. If there was such a time, that time is past.

Yes, we need to teach orthodox Catholic theology, but we must
do so in a way that heals and not just informs.

What follows are three bright-arrow guiding principles that
help me teach teens religion and build a culture of compassion in
the school.

1. Everyone belongs—in your classroom
2. Start with student experience—but don't end there
3. Teach Jesus—and teach like Jesus did

EVERYONE BELONGS—IN YOUR CLASSROOM

> Remember that for Jesus, there is no "other," no one is
> shunned or excluded.[32]
> James Martin SJ

I teach religion and direct student retreats in a Catholic high school. My students, perhaps yours too, reflect a very diverse religious background. I know this because at the beginning of the school year, I ask my students to fill out an information form so that I can get to know them. One question asks about the religious denomination/ affiliation of their parents. As we are a Catholic school, most are Catholic (with varying degrees of church participation). But there are many others as noted below:

My mom is Catholic, my dad is nothing.

My mom is Catholic, I don't know what my dad is, I think he's Catholic.

My mom is Lutheran, my dad is Catholic.

My mom is Catholic, my dad is Christian.

My dad is Anglican, my Mom is Catholic and Buddhist.

My mom and dad believe in God but have no religion.

My mom is Catholic, my dad is Muslim.

Both Muslim.

My mom is Catholic, dad is in between Catholic and nothing.

My mom is Roman Catholic, my dad is United Catholic.

My dad's cholic, my mom's cholic (student couldn't spell "Catholic" or perhaps he meant cranky Catholic).

Anglican, Catholic or something, we're not particular.

My dad is a Christian, I don't think he knows which type, so neither do I.

I don't know, but I'm going to ask them.

My dad is Catholic, I'm not sure about my mom, but she's probably Catholic.

Both Hindu.

Both Bahai.

Both my parents were born again.

My mom's Catholic, dad's an atheist.

My parents are Catholic, I'm an atheist.

My mom says she's Catholic, but I'm not sure.

Native Indian. Aboriginal.

Not religious in any way.

I don't know but my mom is into some spiritual teacher in India.

My parents are Catholic from Ireland.

My mom and dad are Catholic. Both my parents are Filipino.

My mom is Catholic, my dad is still searching.

Sikh for mom and Sikh for dad (Sikh means student).

Islam, both.

Both parents are Ethiopian Orthodox.

Not sure if my family has a religion but I think my grandmother is a little bit of Buddhist.

My mom used to be Anglican, but now they are both Christians.

My dad is Buddhist, I am Taoism.

Dad is Catholic when holidays come.

None.

Not sure.

Complicated.

How do you teach religion in a Catholic school to students with such diverse backgrounds?

Easy! Tell them the truth about religion and tell them which is the true religion. We can do this best with the words of Pope Francis: "True faith is one that makes us more charitable, more merciful, more honest and more humane. It makes us see the other not as an enemy to be overcome, but a brother or sister to be loved, served, helped."[33]

This book promotes the idea that community is formed in a Catholic school by a gospel vision of shared vulnerability that can envelope everyone in the school, no matter how diverse their religious affiliation, or lack thereof. This book maintains that a school with a culture of compassion does not compromise the story and vision of Catholic Christianity; on the contrary, building a culture of compassion in the Catholic school is how Catholic schools today express their catholicity. Failure to do so is un-Catholic because it is un-Christian.

I taught a world religions course to grade elevens. I tried to let the religions speak for themselves. I tried to follow the counsel of Thomas H. Groome in his book, *Will There Be Faith . . .* "the first responsibility of religious educators is to inform and form people in their own particular tradition, giving them a sense of belonging to a spiritual home . . . in a way that diligently discourages sectarianism and bitterness toward "others."[34]

We visited a temple, a church, a mosque and a synagogue. I was very happy, and surprised, that my students discovered a new found inquisitiveness toward the religion they were raised in. And the "nones" developed an appreciation for religion generally. Our world religions course, which some suspect encourages religious relativism, drew our students to greater religious regard.

When biographer Navin B. Chawla asked Mother Teresa whether she tried to convert people, she replied, "Yes, I do convert. I convert you to be a better Hindu, a better Christian, a better Catholic, a better Sikh, a better Muslim."[35]

We do not have to abandon orthodox Christology to show the face of the great includer—a Jesus who is, to Jews, a great Rabbi; to Muslims a great prophet; to Hindus a great spiritual teacher and to Buddhists a great mystic.

> The Catholic Church rejects nothing of what is true and holy in these religions. She has a high regard for the manner of life and conduct, the precepts and doctrines which, although differing in many ways from her own teaching, nevertheless often reflect a ray of truth which enlightens all . . .[36]
>
> Vatican Council II (Nostra Aetate)

> *St. Andrew's is a very good school, the community, which includes staff and students, are all very nice and welcoming. I really like how even though this is a*

*Catholic school, you support all religions. I have had a
very great experience in St. Andrew's so far.*

When we affirm what is true and good in world religions we
are affirming the inclusive and universal Christ who is present there.
A mother asked her 20 year old son:

> *Do you talk about religion with your friends?*
> *Oh, no, we don't do that.*
> *Why not?*
> *One, because we don't want to offend anyone; and two,
> we feel we don't know enough about the subject and are
> afraid of being wrong.*

Religion! What is your gut response? Something that offends
people? Something to fear being wrong about? Pastor and author
Timothy Keller writes that many people today "have come to the
conclusion that religion is one of the greatest sources of misery
and strife in the world."[37] How did religion come to evoke such a
response? One reason is that since the Reformation, in the 16th
century, religion, for many people, has been primarily associated
with defending a set of beliefs against others with a different set of
beliefs. We began to see "them" as "others," not brothers or sisters.
Orthodoxy (right thinking) to the exclusion of orthopraxis (right
living) defined the Christian. This is a truncated Christianity.

Father Joseph F. Girzone wrote *Joshua*, the story of a contem-
porary Jesus with the subtitle: *A Parable for Today*. The book sold
millions. "I was shocked," wrote Girzone, "of the almost universal
response of the public to *Joshua*. It was not just Catholics and Epis-
copalians and Lutherans and Presbyterians but Baptists, Pentecos-
tals, Evangelicals, Jews, Moslems, Hindus, Buddhists, Sikhs, and
not just adults, but children down to nine years old. . . . Jews wrote
and told me they read Joshua and have developed a beautiful relationship with Jesus, and want to follow His way of life privately."[38]

You don't have to call yourself a Christian to have a relationship with Jesus. Jesus doesn't belong to Christians.

"God's Spirit is moving mightily in waves around the world,"
wrote pastor Rick Warren. Church leaders "should stop praying,

"Lord, bless what I'm doing" and start praying, "Lord, help me to do what you are blessing."[39]

Reflecting on the appeal of Jesus as portrayed in the book, Girzone notes that people "are desperately hungering for a relationship with God that can empower them with a new vision of life and heal wounds that have been festering for a lifetime, and renew their zest for living."[40] A relationship with God; a new vision; healed wounds; and enthusiasm for life. Isn't that what religion is about? Isn't that something our students are longing for?

In my class I have students complete the following sentence: The qualities I see in Jesus that I most admire are . . .

The students write:

- His ability to forgive
- His love for children
- How he likes to help people
- His hope for us
- His trust in God the Father
- His compassion for those around him, even the Romans
- His courage
- His passionate love for everyone
- His ability to full-heartedly give his entire life to others
- His determination to do his job

What attracted my students is *how Jesus lived*. They want to learn how to live this way too. This "Way," a name for early Christianity, resonates with our deepest longing. The purpose of information about Jesus is to help students live like Jesus. In the past we put more emphasis on the doctrines that divide us then on the qualities of Jesus that attract us. I suspect if we put more focus on the latter we'd find less to argue about on the former.

A popular word to describe this "way of living" is "spirituality." It is often heard: "I am spiritual, but not religious." Christians should not criticize people for saying "I am spiritual but not religious." Listen to what they are saying. They associate being "religious" with having a set of beliefs and they associate being "spiritual" with having a way of life. They picture religious people arguing with each other about "beliefs"; they picture spiritual people trying to live life in a meaningful way. Christians need to take responsibility for ways they have driven a wedge between the two. It is a separation the high school religious educator needs to reconnect. In Jesus we find the perfect harmony of both.

In New Testament times, the Samaritans had different beliefs than the Jews, and there was mutual hatred for one another. Once, when Jesus and the apostles were travelling through Samaria, the local Samaritans scorned the teaching of the Jewish Jesus. Outraged, James and John asked Jesus: 'Lord, do you want us to command fire to come down from heaven and consume them? Jesus turned and rebuked them' (Luke 9:51). I wonder what Jesus actually said in his rebuke. He might have said: You are being religious but not spiritual.

Would Jesus rebuke much of religion today?

History and current events show that religion often serves our national, cultural, racial or ethnic will, rather than the will of God. Read about or listen to world news. How often is religion coupled with violent conflict between people? Are we surprised that people ask: What good is religion?

Thomas Groome offers a challenge to religion teachers: ". . . all the great religions have the capacity to promote both life and death, love and hate, peace and war. The pages of history are strewn with their mixed legacy. Again, so much depends on how and to what end we "teach them."'[41]

I want every student, whatever their background, to like religion class and to become a better person because of it. I want every student to feel equal and equally valued in class. I want every student to discover God within them.

> I have a dogmatic certainty: God is in every person's life. God is in everyone's life. Even if the life of a person has been a disaster, even if it is destroyed by vices, drugs, or anything else—God is in this person's life. You can, you must try to seek God in every human life.[42]
> Pope Francis

God is in every person's life. Can we approach every person in our class starting from this "certainty?" I have not, and we as church have not always started from this "certainty." Pope Saint John Paul II apologized ninety-nine times for the sins of the Catholic Church— to Jews and Protestants and Muslims and Orthodox Christians and scientists and women and Indigenous people because . . . we did not see God in them.

All of us religious people, and religion teachers especially, must learn and relearn humility. And the ultimate teacher of humility is the one we profess to follow. The divinity of Jesus was displayed by emptying himself of his divinity.

> . . .who, though he was in the form of God, did not re-gard equality with God as something to be exploited, but emptied himself . . .
> Philippians 2: 6–7

This should be the way of the Christian, especially toward those of other faith traditions. The sign that Jesus was of God, true God, one in being with the Father, is that Jesus sought to be identi-fied, in solidarity, with us, all of us. He told his disciples to not be like those who lord it over others (Matthew 20:25): I'm better than you, I'm more worthy than you, I'm above you. Jesus taught that we are most God-like when we are most connected to others and see their dignity and worth.

This is what the parents of your students want. You, as a reli-gious educator, are "in loco parentis"—you take the place of par-ents. What do Muslim parents want for their child? What do Sikh parents want for their child? What do Buddhist parents want for their child? What do Catholic parents want for their child? What do indigenous parents want for their child? They want their child to be a better Muslim, a better Sikh, a better Buddhist, a better Catholic, and they want their child to connect with the sacred traditions and wisdom passed on by their ancestors. God is in every person's life, which is why Catholic schools are not just for Catholics.

Pope Francis calls it the "art of accompaniment," which teach-es us to remove our sandals before the sacred ground of the other.

What does humility look like in the classroom? It looks like listening.

The Church, said Cardinal Luis Antonio Tagle "needs to learn three things from the example of Jesus: humility, respect for others, and the power of silence." "In Jesus," he said, "silence becomes the way of attentive listening, compassion and prayer. It is the way to truth."[43]

Do I belong here? is the first question teens ask when they enter your classroom. Teens need to feel they belong. The good news is that in God they already do. It is the religion teacher who can help them experience this.

START WITH STUDENT EXPERIENCE— BUT DON'T END THERE

Students tell me that a good teacher is deeply interested in the students and in the material being taught. They also say that such a teacher frequently conducts class discussions and does not lecture very much. Almost all of them say that a good teacher relates to them on their level; the teacher does not place herself above them, and they are comfortable talking to her. . . . Students also tell me that they appreciate teachers who make an effort to be entertaining.[44]

William Glasser

The bishops of Canada want to root religious education in the current life experience of today's students. They write:

Meaningful learning is rooted in life experience. Students' personal experiences are the primary resources for understanding life issues and church teaching. . . . The experience portion of each chapter is critical to the unfolding of the lesson. . . . Our understanding of God will have no value if it is not clearly linked to our lives. Any meaningful discussion of God must begin with human experience.[45]

National Office of Religious Education
Canadian Conference of Catholic Bishops

High school religion class is a pastoral ministry which begins with a reflection on our life experience. Otherwise, our understanding of God will have no meaning and no value. Ouch! Strong words.

The bishops of Canada offer the four step process for lesson planning:

Step one: Experience—begin with student experience

Step two: Information—apply theological principles

Step three: Application—consider how these principles change your understanding of your experience

Step four: Action—consider how your new understanding changes your way of living

Here is another way to rephrase the four steps.

Step one: What is the problem?

Step two: What is the spiritual solution?

Step three: How does the solution change the way you think?

Step four: How does the solution change the way you live?

The four step lesson plan is the bishops' way of ensuring that theology serves the pastoral needs of the students. A fuller, deeper and more nuanced explanation of these four "movements" (Groome's preferred term) can be found in chapter eight and nine of a book that should be on every religion teacher's desk: *Will There Be Faith?* by Thomas H. Groome, a world renowned guide in the field of religious education.

I remember once, early in my teaching life, when I spoke a blasphemy, believed heretically and committed a sacrilege. I said something, to myself, that deserved the papal admonition: let him be anathema! That was the day, referring to the girl in the last seat, second row, who never spoke up in class, never contributed, looked rather glum, even indignant, no matter how brilliant my lesson was and how diligently I had prepared it; I said: Does that girl have a soul?

My sin came to consciousness much later when I realized she, indeed, had a soul after all, a heavy weighted soul burdened by unseen traumas and tragedies and afflictions, elusive, perhaps, to all but God. How would I know, I was busy teaching religion. I forgot what Jesus said: Come to me, all you that are weary and are carrying heavy burdens, and I will give you rest (Matthew 11: 28).

Jesus's complaint about his critics is that they did not see God where Jesus saw God. Jesus's critics' biggest complaint was the same: Jesus sees God where God is not.

But Jesus insisted God is with the woman about to be stoned; God is with the tax collector in the tree; God is with the woman at the well and God is with the pagan centurion, the children, the widow, the leper, the man born blind, the paralytic, the outcast, and the "girl with no soul." And I should choke on these words as I write them, for I have not always seen God in my students. Jesus had the most expansive view of God ever!

What was lacking in my assessment was compassion, the very essence of religion. Compassion is a religious way of seeing, more than just a way of believing theological precepts. Jesus said, you have eyes but do not see. He is speaking to me.

In my teaching back then, I skipped the student experience part (step one) and went straight to the theological information part (step two). Consequently, my information went skimming over students' heads and not where I meant to send it—soaring into their hearts. When I look back now I realize that she didn't fail religion, I failed at religious education.

Kids can only take so much "high theology." Over a certain line, they experience it as irrelevant words, stones they stub their toes on, loud noises that disturb them, religious jargon.

"I've learned," said author and pastor Rick Warren, "that most people can't hear until they've first been heard."[46] Cardinal Cupich of Chicago notes: "We're not machines where we can just parrot out the teaching of the church and expect that people are going to be attentive to that . . . no good teacher can get the points across if in fact he or she doesn't know their audience and what their concerns are . . ."[47]

If religion can't speak to life experience, it can't be heard. "Your lesson is very fine," said a student to the religion teacher, "but we are not with it."

Start with student experience because Pope Francis enjoins us to accompaniment.

> We must always consider the person. Here we enter into the mystery of the human being. In life, God accompanies persons, and we must accompany them, starting from their situation. It is necessary to accompany them with mercy.[48]
> Pope Francis

We can't accompany someone when we are a mile ahead of them or off on some distant road. Consider this person whom God is with, and accompany them with mercy, starting with their situation.

Start with student experience because kids are struggling. Students today are more studious, more diligent and more cooperative then they have been in the recent past. On the outside they are exemplary. On the inside they are falling apart.

> *I feel alone. I know all the things I want to tell my mom, but when the time comes, I flake out. I can never say how I feel, even when I rehearse it over and over in my head. I can only tell my dog how I feel, but sometimes it is not enough to hold me together. I fall apart in my room where no one can see my pain.*

> *Because of the media, most people think they are fat, ugly and stupid. I am one of these people.*

> *I'm stressed all the time and have frequent anxiety attacks because I feel burdened by work. My parents don't pressure me. I pressure myself.*

> *I don't tell anyone what I'm feeling. Nobody knows how I am feeling and nobody cares. I sometimes feel there is no God because I feel bad about myself.*

> *I have trouble finding the good in me.*

> *Sometimes I have to go sit in a bathroom stall and silently let my emotions out because I can't hold it until*

*I can get home. If I didn't have my dog and my friends,
I would have been dead a long time ago. I wish I had
confidence.*

*I have no determination for anything. Everything feels
distant and maybe, just maybe . . . if I could just find
myself, maybe then I could be me, be normal.*

*I don't feel real. I have really bad anxiety and a dere-
alization disorder, which causes me to feel like I don't
exist. It sucks because not feeling real makes me feel
anxious and weird.*

*Been having issues with how I see myself physically. It
is taking a toll on my mental health and leads to deci-
sions and habits I regret doing . . . trying to keep your
mind away from negative things is quite difficult.*

*Sometimes I feel positive on a good day, but most days I
consider dying as a better option than being who I am.
I can't tell anyone this stuff or else they will judge me
or pity me. It's hard to act happy but I need to give my
friends the support that I never really had.*

Start with student experience because a young person needs
to express what they are experiencing, and they need someone to
listen. They need to be known. Only by being known, can they
know themselves. Only by being known, can they know what it
means to be known by God.

*In religion class, in my former school, we only learned
about what the Bible and Jesus said by doing crossword
puzzles and watching videos, but now, we actually get
to discuss our feelings on the topic openly.*

Start with student experience because kids don't care how
much you know, until they know how much you care. Starting with
student experience shows kids how much you love them.

And, finally, start with student experience because it brings
fun into the classroom. I have discovered that since religion deals
with personal life issues there should be an equal amount of laughter

and fun to keep a healthy, holy balance. I can be funny, but I'm no comedian. Luckily, most laughter in the class arises from the things kids say and the stories they tell. "I love discussions," students invariably say. And so do I.

Start with student experience, but don't end there. Teach Jesus, and teach like Jesus did.

TEACH JESUS—AND TEACH LIKE JESUS DID.

> What attracted large crowds to Jesus's ministry?
> Jesus did three things with crowds: He loved them,
> he met their needs, and he taught them in interest-
> ing and practical ways. These same three ingredients
> will attract crowds today.[49]
>
> —RICK WARREN, THE PURPOSE DRIVEN CHURCH

1. He loved them.

At the end of a talk I once gave at a religious education conference, a young teacher came to me and told me she always blessed her students at the end of class. It was a short ritual. She prayed over them and blessed them.

"Once," she said, "the bell rang and I was busy at my desk. After some moments I looked up, and my students were all huddled at the door."

"What are you waiting for?" I asked.

"Miss," they replied, "you forgot to give us your blessing."

Kids are dying for a blessing.

Life, for too many kids, does not give them a blessing. Life gives them the opposite. Life gives them a curse. Whereas a blessing builds you up, a curse tears you down. The curse says: You are not good enough, not worthy enough, not perfect enough. This is why they wait at the door for their teacher's blessing.

At the end of Mass the priest says: May Almighty God bless you in the name of the Father, and the Son, and the Holy Spirit. Go in peace, glorifying the Lord by your life.

Loving others with no strings; to really want the best for them, unselfishly; this is difficult. It is difficult because we need love ourselves. We cannot give what we have not received. How can you draw from an empty well?

> Everyone who drinks of this water will be thirsty again, but those who drink of the water that I will give them will never be thirsty. The water that I will give will become in them a spring of water gushing up to eternal life.
> John 4:13

Where to get that water?

"Our life," said Henri J. M. Nouwen, "is full of brokenness—broken relationships, broken promises, broken expectations. How can we live with that brokenness without becoming bitter and resentful except by returning again and again to God's faithful presence in our lives."[50] Returning again and again to God's faithful presence in our life is where we receive the love we give to our students.

Teaching is a vocation, a call from God, sustained by God. A classroom is a place we meet thirsty souls. The water kids drink is the water of our competitive, comparing and score-keeping culture, and so they are thirsty again. In religion class we offer the water that Jesus gives them, the infinitely flowing stream of God's love for us "welling up to eternal life."

2. He met their needs

When your lesson plan starts with students' experience, you are meeting students' needs, as Jesus did. Adolescents need to know that other teens struggle as they do. The new self-consciousness of adolescence often translates as: I'm the only one who feels this, thinks this, and is going through this. The relief they have when they discover that they are "normal," turns distress into de-stress. A de-stressed student is ready to learn. As one student told me: "Now that I have friends, my grades are going up."

Only if a child feels right can he think right.[51]
Haim Ginott

William Glasser, author of *The Quality School,* lists a young person's needs as follows:

- Belonging: feeling connected and accepted
- Empowerment: feeling significant in the eyes of others
- Fun: feeling joy
- Love: feeling affirmed and respected
- Freedom: feeling free to express thoughts and feelings

As significant as *why* we should start with student experience, is *how* we should start. Don't stand before a class of twenty-six students and say, "Well, what do you think of X, Y, Z?" Most of the time they are not consciously thinking of the topics you wish to teach, and most are unwilling to venture across the thin ice of other students' judgements by offering an answer out loud to everyone. This is when you have to "prime the pump," or, as I call it, "provoke a response." Provoking a response is easy. It's the no-stress-grab-your-attention method found in teen magazines and church youth group resources.

Here is my list:

1. True or False
2. Agree or Disagree
3. Choose the answer closest to your own thoughts
4. Put in order of importance
5. Complete the sentence
6. "Survey says" anonymous comments read aloud
7. Rank the following from 1—don't like, to 5—like a lot

Provoking a response is the mental icebreaker that gets a lesson started. Provoking a response helps us begin the "life" part of the lesson plan, as in Thomas Groome's approach to religious education: "Life to faith to life." Provoking a response is the grist which can segue into a big circle discussion where "no one can speak unless you have the pillow, so raise your hand to get the pillow."

If you start by listening to students, you end with students wanting to listen to you. You met their needs, now you need to teach in practical and interesting ways, as Jesus did.

3. He taught them in interesting and practical ways.

We are interested in answers to questions we are asking and solutions to problems we are having. Why then, in many religion classes, are we giving them answers to questions they are not asking and solutions to problems they are not having?

Here are the problems they are trying to solve:

- *So many beauty standards women "have to follow."*
- *Last year I didn't like me. This year I hate me.*
- *I struggle to find the good in me.*
- *I lost myself.*
- *I hate my body.*
- *I'm always stressed if I am not good enough.*
- *Having people yell at me for messing up in a sport is killing me.*
- *I wish I wasn't so mean sometimes.*
- *I'm starting to think I hate myself.*
- *I don't feel real.*
- *Trying to keep your mind away from negative things is quite difficult.*
- *I wear a mask to protect myself.* (Editor's Note: good if it protects against the viral pandemic, not good if it's a figurative mask hiding your true self.)
- *I feel more love-hungry. I want to be loved by someone I like.*
- *I feel quite empty about myself because of the stupid things I have done.*
- *All the girls hate each other and all the boys are on drugs.*
- *I need help.*

From an analysis of these problems to solve we can derive the questions to answer:

- Who am I?
- Is life worth living?
- Who is my neighbor?
- Does suffering have meaning?
- What is my worth?
- What is love?
- How can one love one's self?
- Is forgiveness possible?
- Why do I feel the way I do?
- Why am I so stressed?
- How can I find inner peace?

Students today are interested in Church teaching when applied in practical ways to their life. Pastor Rick Warren recommends less "ought-to" messages and more "how-to" messages. The truth they are looking for is the truth that gives them relief. "All problems are psychological, but all solutions are spiritual," says Dr. Thomas Hora.[52] How can the religion teacher respond to these psychological problems with spiritual solutions?

What follows are two topic examples we can offer our students. They will find these topics interesting and practical because these are the issues they deal with—almost daily. The two topics I have chosen, among many, are:

1. Anxiety
2. Self-worth

> Without the reassuring experience of God the world is perceived to be potentially hostile.[53]
> Fr. Thomas Keating

1. Anxiety

Anxiety is all the buzz, and commonly touted as the world's most pervasive mental health problem. In a June 11, 2020 news item, National Public Radio reports that the *Women's Preventive Services Initiative* wants doctors and other health care providers to screen all adult and adolescent women and girls for anxiety disorders beginning at age 13. This news item is about a woman's initiative, but boys and men struggle with anxiety as well. If healthcare practitioners are encouraged to broach the subject of anxiety with every teenager, I think religious educators need to do likewise. Is there a spiritual solution to the problem of anxiety?

Assessing the level of stress and anxiety in teens today can lead to two questions: What is happening to teens and what is not happening to teens that accounts for the high level of stress and anxiety in their lives? Most people focus on the first question because it is easier to assess what did happen rather than what didn't happen. When asking: What is happening to teens?, the obvious targets are often cited: social media, a highly competitive culture, economic insecurity, strained family attachment, global instability. And the winner is . . . Social Media.

> *Social media makes it hard for me and I think most of the grade to love ourselves.*

Andrea, in grade eight, reflected on this theme in an essay she wrote on *Dealing With Hard Times.* With her permission, I include it here:

> We go through tough times often nowadays. It's very intriguing to see how much 'tough times' have changed over the past decades. In the 80's, kids my age would go through 'tough times' by worrying if they could afford the new Cabbage Patch doll or the Atari gaming system. Nowadays, things have definitely changed. We see beautiful people and we wonder if we are good enough. We see influencers and we strive to be like them. We think that millions of people like them, so maybe if we are like them, people will like us. We get negative towards ourselves and we get disappointed that we aren't like them.

Most youth use the internet and social media in creative, productive, and sometimes life-saving ways. The skills of digital natives are envied by digital immigrants—like me. It is a good thing to own cutting-edge devices, but it is a bad thing to be owned by our devices. It is a marvelous tool, but it's just a tool.

Besides what is happening in the lives of teens that triggers anxiety, what is missing that needs to happen? Mark W. Baker writes that anxiety is not the problem, but not having a way to make sense of it is. He conducted a study with those who are "intrinsically religious" and those who are not religious at all. He discovered that if you were religious or not you had the same amount of anxiety. But he also discovered that those who identified as religious were able to "return to a state of happiness much faster than those who don't have a personally meaningful religion to help them do that."[54] Religion does not prevent anxiety, it helps one deal with it. Without a spiritual path, stress becomes distress. This is stated beautifully by one student on his retreat evaluation:

> *Everything is going to turn out okay. There are no real stresses in life; love cures and brings new life to everything. Thank you so much for doing this retreat.*

How do you make sense of anxiety? You put it into a bigger perspective, the perspective of faith. God is with us, we are in good hands.

Up half the night worrying about the state of the Church, Pope John XXIII finally came to his senses: Wait a minute, this isn't my church, this is God's church. God! Take care of your church! Goodnight!

And the Pope slept well.

Cyrille experienced the dark night of an anxious soul, but she went through it. Her religion enabled her to do so. Not without pain and not without questioning her faith. But as she said in her talk: "It also helps me to know that there is always Someone there for me—to listen, to rant to, to talk to, or even to blame when things go wrong. Knowing this has helped me through this dark place, because who knows what I could have done or what would have happened to me if I didn't know Someone was always there for me."

What is not happening in the lives of many teenagers, is having someone who can show them a spiritual path through the anxiety they are experiencing. Knowing that we are not alone on this path helps us travel it. Without knowing this, youth experience an existential homelessness. That is cause for anxiety and depression in anyone.

The great spiritual director, Saint Francis de Sales, has some wise advice for those bedeviled with anxiety. "Disquietude" (worry, anxiety), he says, "is the greatest evil that happens to the soul except sin." Anxiety arises, says the saint, from an immoderate desire to be free of it. Anxiety about your anxiety makes it worse. Birds, he explains, immoderately trying to free themselves from nets, entangle themselves even more. So what should you do?

> ". . . before all things place your spirit in a state of repose and tranquility, calm your judgement and your will. And, then, quite softly and gently, pursue the end of your desire, taking in order the means which will be suitable. And when I say quite softly, I do not wish to say negligently, but without worry, trouble and disquietude. Otherwise, in place of giving effect to your desire, you spoil everything, and will embarrass yourself very greatly.
>
> Saint Francis de Sales

For Saint Francis de Sales, immoderately fighting one's anxiety, only empowers it. How can we be at peace with what is disturbing our peace?

The idea that painful feelings reveal that there-is-something-wrong with-me, misses what the soul has to teach us when we go through tough times. Religion, the servant of the soul, can offer wise and compassionate guidance in this process, and a community of fellow seekers to go through it with.

When Johann Hari was a teenager he saw a doctor for his anxiety and depression that he described as a "pain leaking out of me." The doctor informed Johann that some people naturally get a chemical imbalance in their head and that he was one of them. Drugs were the prescription. The drugs worked, for a while. Eventually higher doses were needed. For thirteen years Johann was taking the legally maximum dose of anti anxiety/depression drugs.

Then, Johann set out on a journey to find the answer to two gnawing questions: Why, after thirteen years of being medicated, am I still in pain; and why is depression and anxiety a growing worldwide phenomenon?

In his Ted Talk: *This could be why you're depressed or anxious*,[55] the result of his quest, Johann Hari gives due recognition to the biological causes of depression and anxiety and to what medication can effect, but claims that most factors causing depression and anxiety are not in our biology but are factors in the way we live. Alongside the chemical solutions, there are other solutions we need to know about. These solutions are about our deeper need to belong, to have meaning and purpose in life, and to envision a future that makes sense. We need to talk less about chemical imbalances, he says, and more about the imbalances in the way we live.

One imbalance he highlights is loneliness. "We are the loneliest society in human history," he maintains, as people no longer feel close to anyone. We need to be known and connected to others on a deep level.

> In a spoken poem there is a line that says, "If a kid breaks in school and no one around chooses to hear, do they make a sound?" That's how I feel. I feel alone.

A second imbalance Hari highlights is what he calls "junk values" which starve us of nutrition for our spirit, like "junk food" does for our body. Junk values incline us to look for happiness in the wrong places—wealth, prestige and things outside ourselves, rather than loving connection with others.

In his quest, Johann Hari discovered that the pain he felt as a teenager was more than just a biological malady with a chemical solution. It was a signal with a message to attend to his deep spiritual needs.

Could this be what is happening to our youth? Are they receiving only direction in how to *manage* their struggles rather than finding the *message* and the deeper *meaning* in the struggles they are having? Is much of their anxiety a distress call for the One who is close to the brokenhearted? I think so. The quest that Johann Hari undertook is the quest that religion class and class retreats should facilitate in the lives of our students. It is the accompaniment our students desire.

2. Self worth

Mark W. Baker writes: "Self-esteem is based upon two things: feeling useful and feeling valuable. You feel useful based on encouragement for your accomplishments and hard work. You feel valuable based on being loved and accepted for who you are. It is important to have both of these in life. But one cannot replace the other."[56]

I explain to my students, as well, the distinction between self-esteem, which is based on how you feel about yourself, which can go up and down; and self-worth which can never go down for it is based on God's love for you, which is constant and eternal. Good principle to follow: Base your self-esteem on your self-worth.

Youth need to feel valuable for who they are, and that is the central message of healthy religion—God loves you and always will. Youth also need to feel useful by their accomplishments, but there is something in our culture undermining that.

Sarah Swafford, in her book, *Emotional Virtue—a guide to drama free relationships*, calls it "The World's Idea of Perfect."[57] Kids are filled with anxiety because they feel pressured to be perfect according to "The World's Idea of Perfect" and to present that image which "the world (and seemingly everyone else) judges you by." In comes the competition and comparison, out goes the confidence.

Everyone expects you to be perfect.

If you ever want to be noticed, you have to be pretty and skinny, but that's not me.

I put too much pressure on myself and struggle to find the good in me.

Pressured, I feel like I can't decide for myself, I'm always monitored, self-conscious.

*I hate how I look, behave, everything. I lost myself . . .
had to create multiple personalities beside different
groups, BUT I'M DONE PRETENDING.*

*I feel like I'm always being judged by people better in
every way.*

*I put too much pressure on myself to do well. I feel that
I have to do the best even if I know I don't have to.*

What will help youth today is religion class with lessons on identity and worth, the value of which is not conditioned by the world's idea of perfect, but is given to us as daughters and sons of a God who loves us unconventionally.

What do you call helping young people who struggle with anxiety, stress and low self-esteem? Some people call it mental health care. I call it spiritual direction. The original counselling was spiritual counselling. People had, and some today have, spiritual directors. That is what a high school religion teacher is, an adolescent spiritual director. We do group therapy.

Saint Thomas Aquinas, in the Middle Ages, found that Aristotelian philosophy helped him understand religious truth. Today, the social sciences are doing the same. The social sciences can help us understand the teaching and healing ministry of Jesus, and help us teach and heal like Jesus did.

Religion teachers do not replace counsellors and psychologists and social workers. We work together. Mark W. Baker Ph.D. is a licensed clinical psychologist, and the author of the internationally acclaimed, *Jesus the Greatest Therapist Who Ever Lived*. He writes, "For over twenty years I have been interested in the study of both theology and psychology. I have found each discipline to deepen my understanding of the other. I have never ceased to be amazed at the points of agreement between spiritual and emotional principles that facilitate health."[58]

It was the psychologist Sigmund Freud who sowed seeds of suspicion in religious people when he spoke of religion as childlike wishes or an illusion that people use to deal with life's trials. But it was Freud's student, C. G. Jung, referring to his patients in the second half of life, wrote: "Among all my patients . . . it is safe to say that every one of them fell ill because he had lost that which the living religions of every age have given to their followers, and none of them has really been healed who did not regain his religious outlook."[59]

There are rainy-day-lessons, last-block-of-the-day lessons, the day before holiday lessons, Friday lessons, and lessons when kids are "just not there." There are fact lessons: How is the pope elected, name the liturgical seasons of the year and these are the bible stories you need to know. There are catechetical lessons straight out of the catechism. All these lessons we try to make "interesting." But students will starve without a feast of lessons that satisfy the hunger in their hearts and the dilemmas in their heads. Once you see, as a religion teacher, how much kids appreciate lessons that instill hope in their present struggles, you will never go back to a "dryly propositional and uninspiring catechesis."

As religion teachers, when we stand before our class, we should stand as Jesus did before the crowds.

> When he saw the crowds, he had compassion for them, because they were harassed and helpless, like sheep without a shepherd. Then he said to his disciples, "The harvest is plentiful, but the laborers are few . . ."
> Matthew 9: 36–37

This book is a call to Catholic school educators to attend to the plentiful harvest with the compassion of Jesus. We do not have to wait for a "teachable moment" to do this. Adolescence is a teachable moment.

We start our lesson plan (step one) with student experience. We follow (step two) with the Gospel and the teachings of the Church, what Thomas Groome calls the Christian Story and Vision. We proceed (step three) by asking how the story and vision has changed the way you understand your life experience. For step three I ask my students to answer this question in an essay—which is a glimpse of their story.

> Use fewer examinations, fewer quizzes, and more essay assignments. You don't know anything about a subject

until you can put your knowledge into some kind of expression.[60]

Wayne C. Booth

Reading their essay and offering my written reflections on what they have written, is another way to connect with my students. They look forward to my "feedback," and I look forward to reading their words.

Adolescence is a great adventure but also a perilous journey. As the finishing touches were being completed on this book, Svenya, in grade eight, wrote the following in an essay on *Friendship*. With her permission, it is included below. Seeing God, in the life of a young teenager, reminds me how blessed I am to be a religion teacher.

> When there are times in my life that I feel left out, hurt, or even friendless, I know I can talk to God to help me get through. God has, and will forever be there for me in times of joy, and in times of sorrow. In my opinion, it is important, especially in adolescent years, to be close with God because he is the one who guides us, and if we listen to him and our hearts, we will make the right choices in our lives. I know I will be tempted to do the wrong thing in the next few years ahead of me, but as long as I stay strong and listen to God, I will be rewarded the strength to resist.

Finally, step four: How has this unit changed your life going forward. For step four, we pray.

We gather in a circle and light candles which we place around a crucifix on a cloth in the middle of the room. We pass a candle around and share what we have learned. We read scripture, listen to praise and worship music, and give each other affirmations, which we call bouquets. Then we place the essays around the cloth as a sign of offering our life to God's grace. Prayer is what enables us to live the lessons we learn.

Coming to know God and coming to know ourselves, advance along the same path. This is beautifully expressed in the little classic on prayer: *Praying Our Experiences* by Joseph F. Schmidt FSC.

This means that in prayer we are neither on the one hand dialoguing with an outside source who utters messages from without nor are we simply talking to ourselves. We are reaching deeply into ourselves and sensing more clearly that we are in God's knowledge and love. We are discovering the Divine within us. We are experiencing ourselves and our lives as uttered by God, and we listen.[61]

Joseph F. Schmidt FSC

Such are the steps, of the four step lesson plan, which we will start all over again, in the next unit, in religion class.

FINAL THOUGHTS

It is a common matter of observation . . . the better is the life of the preacher, the greater is the fruit he bears, however undistinguished his life may be, however small his rhetoric and however ordinary is his instruction. For it is the warmth that comes from the living spirit that clings, whereas the other kind of preacher will produce very little profit, however sublime be his style and his instruction.

St. John of the Cross

By now you might have guessed that I don't put too much stock in "completing and covering the curriculum." Behold, the curriculum is sitting in front of you. One good lesson that warms the heart is worth a hundred lessons that merely skim the head and are here today and gone tomorrow. The central principle is this: Religious education is a lifelong endeavor. What they need now, they need now. What they need later, they need later. It is impossible to give them now what they need later, and it is woefully regrettable to miss giving what they need now. I was hungry and you did not feed me; I was thirsty and received nothing to drink.

You are not teaching the curriculum, you are teaching the kids. Use the curriculum to teach the kids but don't use the kids to teach the curriculum.

I want to teach what we believe as Catholics in a way that sheds light on the problems and dilemmas that perplex teens today. I want my religion class to be assessed more by the quality of the learning experience than by the quantity of information imparted. I want kids to think of the religion teacher as someone who wants to know them. I want them to experience religion class as the one place where they matter as much as the lesson plan matters. I want to teach the best way as much as I want to teach The Way.

I enjoy religion class. Not only do we learn about our religion but we learn about ourselves as well.

I feel safe and secure and I feel that my religion teachers are people I can trust and go to about my faith or when I have questions.

I think religion class has really helped me find who I am and has made me really think about myself and the people around me. It has helped me find my faith and has brought me closer to God.

I really enjoy religion class. I myself do not belong to a religion but I believe religion class has had a positive influence on me.

The lessons we learn can be taken and applied to many situations in life.

The sense of security religion class creates is what keeps students coming back year after year. It is what makes our school unique. It is what makes our school something closer to home.

Thank you for teaching me this year, not only about religion, but about life. Thank you for helping me find myself and God. I couldn't have done it without you, and I believe I wouldn't be who I am now, if it weren't for you.

Everyday I look forward to religion class.

Don't expect your tightly argued reasons and neat apologetics to produce faith. Faith is not a production. Religious truth is not detached facts that critics imagine. Religious truth is knowing-in-relationship. You are inviting students into a relationship with God, with others and with their deepest self. Relationships take time. Spiritual development has moments of great joy, but it is also, like all meaningful relationships, a long and painstaking process. Realize that in religion class the message-you-teach, and the message-you-are, are so entwined that kids don't see a difference. They read you like a gospel.

Announce the gospel but be patient when the response is a blank stare. Quidquid recipitur ad modum recipientis recipitur, said Saint Thomas Aquinas. Whatever is received into something is received according to the condition of the receiver. Understanding, according to Aquinas, is a mysteriously passive process; something received, not strictly from one's own intellectual effort. "Truth which is merely told," writes religious scholar William Barclay, "is quick to be forgotten; truth which is discovered lasts a lifetime."[62] The old adage says as much: When the student is ready, the teacher will appear. Find out what they are ready for, and then appear. Teens are in various stages of readiness. The gospel we announce may sprout roots or it may lie dormant for a long winter. But the Lord assures us that the seed "will not return to me empty, but will accomplish what I desire and achieve the purpose for which I sent it" (Isaiah 55:11). Teaching faith is an act of faith.

Announce the gospel with enthusiasm, but do not be surprised if your students are more intrigued by the fact that you are personally passionate than by what you are passionate about. Some see your passion as a personality quirk they can mimic in jest. About your message some think: God loves us . . . really . . . come on . . . whatever. Adolescence is an explosion of awareness and what a teacher says is set alongside a vast plethora of images and voices and impressions that strike them daily, thousands in social media alone. Without a bank of life experience to draw upon, they have little to compare and contrast this present input. And this is why adolescence lasts at least a full decade, giving one the time to set in place the foundation of a real and my-very-own person. Know this, however. As a high school religion teacher, you are doing better than you think. You are your worst critic, not the kids. They admire you more than you realize.

It is more important to teach kids to think religiously than to think about religion. To utilize the familiar adage: if you give a student a religious concept, they remember for a day; but if you teach them how to see religiously, they begin a life long spiritual journey.

For students to see religiously they need a mentor who can listen to their story with ears tuned to a religious heart. As an adult you know this is happening when you see hints of God, signs of grace, stirrings of faith and a longing that is holy in the teenager before you. And your students will see in your eyes "a mirror in which they discover themselves" (Glasser).

When I say teaching religion is the hardest subject, I invariably get the following response: Yes, and that is because kids today are secular, materialistic, post-modern, digitally obsessed moral relativists. Not so! Give the kids a chance to speak. It is a humbling experience to discover the depth of their concerns and how concisely they express them. Kids today want to tell you their struggles; they want to be known by you; and then, and only then, they want to know: What do you think?

From my experience very few adults in the school understand the spiritual needs of youth as revealed in this book. This is not a criticism. They are teaching math, history, science, literature and physics. They are coaching teams and trying to win the district title. They are rehearsing for the opening night and the spring concert. They are grading papers, writing report cards, going to meetings and completing their professional development plans. They are busy.

But you are the religion teacher. Can they bare their soul to you? Can you take that message to the staff meeting? Can you advocate for youth when time and treasure is being allocated for retreats and school liturgies? I've done this. I've taught religion and directed retreats in three Catholic high schools in the USA and Canada. I spoke out. I advocated for youth. I ruffled some feathers. I feel good about that. Advocating for the needs of youth is part of your job description. Who do you think you are working for?

From my present vantage point, one thing is clear to me; spiritual growth and development is a life-long process and it has little to do with our own achievement and all to do with surrendering to the love God has for us and making that love the very core of our worth and the motive of our life. How hard is that?

Well, I can only answer for myself. I've had experiences of God's love for me. I know what that is like, but then I forget it. In prayer I have experienced the peace of God's presence, but then I get distracted. I seem to operate on a peaceful loving steady keel, until a minor crisis happens, and deep egoic regions within me take over and I say and do things I later regret. How deep is my faith?

For a person who has been to Catholic elementary school, high school, university and graduate school, and who has taught in Catholic schools for the better part of four decades, in short, been exposed to all things Catholic all my life, and to always come back to the realization that I'm only just beginning, this flies in the face of society's ideal of growth, progress and the accumulated accolades that make for a very impressive resume.

Yet . . . I'm beginning to see that only when I am humble, knowing my own weakness, realizing my need for God, feeling empty, only then do I become compassionate, gentle and less critical of others. The spiritual "trick," it seems to me, is to stay humble.

If the journey of an elder like me, who has been around the block more than just a few times, and is still seeking, what can I expect from yearlings in my classroom mesmerized by the bells and mirrors and flashes of this culture and the siren sounds of cyberspace. Can I convince them that what they are looking for is not there. Why, they have only begun to look! I was young once. Can I turn them in a new direction or can I just sow a seed? As I ponder this question there is one thing I know I can give them—a good experience of religion class. And I know this is happening when I see their souls light up their faces and hear them say, "Religion is my favorite class."

Chapter Endnotes

1. Popularly attributed to American poet John Ciardi.
2. Merton, *New Seeds of Contemplation*, 36.
3. Chittister, *Scarred by Struggle*, 40.
4. Benner, *The Gift of Being Yourself*, 26.
5. Lindbergh, *Gift From the Sea*, 32.
6. van Breemen, *The God Who Won't Let Go*, 141–142.
7. Delio, *The Unbearable Wholeness of Being*, 87.
8. van Breemen, *The God Who Won't Let Go*, 12.
9. Rohr, "Negative Capability," para 1.
10. Rolheiser, *Wrestling with God*, 104.
11. Moore, *Dark Nights of the Soul*, XVI–XVIII.
12. Barron, *New King*, 7.
13. Keane, *James Martin Essential Writings*, 132–133.
14. Tobias et al., *A Parliament of Souls*, 204–205.
15. Miller, *The Holy See's Teaching*, VII.
16. Feheney, *From Ideal to Action*, 6.
17. Baker, *Overcoming Shame*, 43–44.
18. World Economic Forum on YouTube, "Charter For Compassion."
19. Conroy, *The Death of Santini*, 39.
20. The BioSpiritual Institute, "Why Pay Attention to Feelings," para 6.
21. Tournier, *To Understand Each Other*, 8.
22. Hersch, *A Tribe Apart*, 358–359.
23. Hersch, *A Tribe Apart*, 365.
24. Baker, *Overcoming Shame*, 44.
25. Miller, *The Holy See's Teaching*, 33–34.
26. Miller, *The Holy See's Teaching*, 63.
27. Pope Francis, General Audience, 2/19/2014.
28. Crabb, *Connecting*, XII.
29. Mulligan, *A Pastor's Journal*, 152.
30. USCCB, *National Directory*, 201.
31. Greeley, *The Great Mysteries*, VII–VIII.
32. Spadaro et al., *A Big Heart*, 141.

33. Pope Francis, Holy Mass, 04/09/2017.
34. Groome, *Will There Be Faith?*, 1.
35. Chawla, "I Convert You," para 3.
36. Pope Paul VI, Nostra Aetate, 10/28/1965.
37. Keller, *The Prodigal God*, 75.
38. Girzone, *Never Alone*, 10.
39. Warren, *The Purpose Driven Church*, 15.
40. Girzone, *Never Alone*, 10.
41. Groome, *Will There Be Faith?*, 11.
42. Spadaro et al., *A Big Heart*, 50.
43. NCR Editorial Staff, "Evangelization," para 9.
44. Glasser, *The Quality School*, 66.
45. CCCB, *Teacher's Manual*, 13.
46. Warren, *The Purpose Driven Church*, 40.
47. McElwee, "Cupich Says," 2/9/2018.
48. Spodaro et al., *A Big Heart*, 141.
49. Warren, *The Purpose Driven Church*, 208.
50. DeMuth, *Authentic Parenting*, 156.
51. Ginott, *Teacher & Child*, 69.
52. Hora, *Beyond The Dream*, xxiv.
53. Keating, *Intimacy With God*, 75.
54. Baker, *Spiritual Wisdom*, 173.
55. Hari, "Why You're Depressed."
56. Baker, *Spiritual Wisdom*, 107.
57. Swafford, *Emotional Virtue*, 19.
58. Baker, *Jesus, The Greatest Therapist*, XIII.
59. Hull, *Works of Jung Volume 11*, 334.
60. Booth, *Vocation Of A Teacher*, 215.
61. Schmidt, *Praying Our Experiences*, 33–34.
62. Barclay, *The Mind of Jesus*, 95.

Appendix 1

10 Takeaways from the *Directory For Catechesis*

Pontifical Council for the Promotion of the New Evangelization
2020

In 1965, the Vatican Council called for a directory "for the catechetical instruction of the Christian people in which the fundamental principles of this instruction. . .will be dealt with." The *General Catechetical Directory* was published in 1971 and revised in 1997. It encouraged national directories as well; in 1979, The US bishops obliged with the *National Catechetical Directory*. It was revised in 2005. On March 23, 2020, Pope Francis approved the new *Directory for Catechesis*, from which the following quotes, relevant to the contents of this book, are taken.

1. #51 The Church is called to proclaim her primary truth, which is the love of Christ. . .The practice of mercy is already itself an authentic catechesis; it is catechesis in action, an eloquent testimony for believers and nonbelievers alike and a manifestation of the bond between orthodoxy and orthopraxy. . .

2. #113 . . .the catechist is. . .an expert in the art of accompaniment, has educational expertise, is able to listen and enter into the dynamic of human growth, becomes a traveling companion with patience and a sense of gradualness, in docility to the action of the Spirit. . .The catechist. . .knows the joys and hopes of human beings, their sadness and distress and is able to situate them in relation to the Gospel of Jesus.

3. #144 Finally, in ecumenical contexts and those of religious pluralism, care should be taken to familiarize catechists with the essential elements of the life and theology of the other Churches and Christian communities and of the other religions, so that, with respect for everyone's identity, dialogue may be authentic and fruitful.

4. #146 . . .adequate consideration should be given to psychology, sociology, pedagogy, the sciences of education, formation, and communication. The Church feels called upon to engage with these sciences for the sake of the valuable contribution they can make both to the formation of catechists and to catechetical activity itself. Theology and the human sciences, in fact, can enrich each other.

5. #179 . . .the work of the catechist consists in finding and drawing attention to the signs of God's action already present in the lives of persons and, by using these as an example, present the Gospel as a transformative power for the whole of existence, to which it will give full meaning.

6. #180 . . .psychology also has an important value, above all because it helps one to grasp the motivational dynamics, the structure of the personality, the elements relating to problems and pathologies, the different stages of development and developmental tasks, the dynamics of religious maturation and the experiences that open human beings to the mystery of the sacred.

7. #199 Catechesis, following the example of Jesus, helps to illuminate and interpret the experiences of life in the light of the Gospel.

8. #219 . . .young people. . .feel very keenly the need for authentic relationships. . . The catechist is called to awaken within the

group the experience of community as the most coherent expression of the Church's life, which finds its most visible form in the celebration of the Eucharist.

9. #252 The Church, manifesting the same solicitude as Jesus, wants to listen to young people with patience, understand their anxieties, have a true heart-to-heart dialogue, (and) accompany them in discerning their life plan.

10. #345 Catechesis. . .is to take care. . .to expound clearly and with charity the doctrine of the Catholic faith "respecting in a particular way the order of the hierarchy of truths and avoiding expressions and ways of presenting doctrine which would be an obstacle to dialogue.

Appendix 2

10 Takeaways from
Fratelli Tutti
(All Brothers and Sisters)

Encyclical Letter on Fraternity
and Social Friendship
2020

In 2013, Pope Francis issued the encyclical letter Evangelii gaudium (The joy of the Gospel) on the Church as a community of missionary disciples; in 2015, Laudato si (Praise Be to You) concerning care for the planet; in 2016 Amoris laetitia (The joy of love) on love within the family; in 2020 Fratelli tutti, from which the following quotes, relevant to the contents of this book, are taken.

1. #30 Isolation and withdrawal into one's own interests are never the way to restore hope and bring about renewal. Rather, it is closeness; it is the culture of encounter. Isolation, no; closeness, yes. Culture clash, no; culture encounter, yes.

2. #42 Digital media can also expose people to the risk of addiction, isolation and a gradual loss of contact with concrete

reality, blocking the development of authentic interpersonal relationships.

3. #85 If we go to the ultimate source of that love which is the very life of the triune God, we encounter in the community of the three divine Persons the origin and perfect model of all life in society.

4. #86 . . .it is important that catechesis and preaching speak more directly and clearly about the social meaning of existence, the fraternal dimension of spirituality, our conviction of the inalienable dignity of each person, and our reasons for loving and accepting all our brothers and sisters.

5. #111 The human person, with his or her inalienable rights, is by nature open to relationship. Implanted deep within us is the call to transcend ourselves through an encounter with others.

6. #216 To speak of a "culture of encounter" means that we, as a people, should be passionate about meeting others, seeking points of contact, building bridges, planning a project that includes everyone.

7. #217 What is important is to create processes of encounter, processes that build a people that can accept differences. Let us arm our children with the weapons of dialogue! Let us teach them to fight the good fight of the culture of encounter.

8. #276 And in imitation of Mary, the Mother of Jesus, we want to be a Church that serves, that leaves home and goes forth from its places of worship, goes forth from its sacristies, in order to accompany life, to sustain hope, to be the sign of unity. . .to build bridges, to break down walls, to sow seeds of reconciliation.

9. #277 Yet we Christians are very much aware that if the music of the Gospel ceases to resonate in our very being, we will lose the joy born of compassion, the tender love born of trust, the capacity for reconciliation that has its source in our knowledge that we have been forgiven and sent forth.

10. #281 God does not see with his eyes, God sees with his heart. And God's love is the same for everyone, regardless of religion.

Contact the Authors

Danny Brock
domano@telus.net

Cyrille Santos
cyrilles.info@gmail.com

Bibliography

Baker, Mark W. *Jesus The Greatest Therapist Who Ever Lived*. New York: Harper Collins, 2007.

———. *Overcoming Shame*. Eugene, Oregon: Harvest House, 2018.

———. *Spiritual Wisdom for a Happier Life*. Grand Rapids, MI: Revell, 2017.

Baars, Conrad. *Born Only Once*. Chicago: Franciscan Herald, 1975.

Barclay, William. *The Mind of Jesus*. New York: Harper & Row, 1960.

Barron Bp., Robert. *New King for a New Kingdom*. Fenton, MO: Creative Communications, 2012.

Benner, David G. *The Gift of Being Yourself*. Downers Grove, IL: InterVarsity, 2004.

BioSpiritual Institute. "Why Pay Attention To Feelings? Seven Fundamentals About Body Knowing and Learning." https://www.biospiritual.org/why-biospiritual-focusing/why-pay-attention-to-feelings/.

Booth, Wayne C. *The Vocation of a Teacher: Rhetorical Occasions, 1967–1988*. University of Chicago Press, 1988.

Canadian Conference of Catholic Bishops. *Stand By Me, Teacher's Manual*. Ottawa, ON: CCCB. 1996.

Chawla, Navin B. "I convert you to be a better Hindu, a better Christian, a better Muslim." https://economictimes.indiatimes.c om/blogs/et-commen tary/73995/.

Chittister, Joan D. *Scarred by Struggle, Transformed by Hope*. Grand Rapids, MI: Wm. B. Eerdmans, 2003.

Conroy, Pat. *The Death of Santini*. New York: Doubleday, 2013.

Crabb, Larry. *Connecting*. Nashville, TN: Word, 1997.

Delio, Ilia. *The Unbearable Wholeness of Being*. Maryknoll, New York: Orbis, 2013.

DeMuth, Mary. *Authentic Parenting in a Postmodern Culture*. Eugene, OR: Harvest House, 2007.

Feheney, FPM, J. Matthew, ed. *From Ideal to Action*. Dublin, Ireland: Veritas, 1998.

Ginott, Haim. *Teacher & Child*. New York: Avon, 1975.

Girzone, Joseph F. *Never Alone*. New York: Doubleday, 1994.

Glasser, William. *The Quality School*. New York: Harper and Row, 1990.

Greeley, Andrew M. *The Great Mysteries*. Lanham, Maryland: Sheed & Ward, 2003.

Groome, Thomas H. *Will There Be Faith?* New York: HarperCollins, 2011.

Hari, Johann. "This could be why you're depressed or anxious." July 2019. https://www.ted.com/talks/johann_hari_this_could_be_why_you_re_depressed_or_anxious.

Hersch, Patricia. *A Tribe Apart*. New York: Ballantine, 1998.

Hora, Thomas. *Beyond The Dream*. New York: Crossroad, 1996.

Hull, R.F.C., translator. *The Collected Works of C. G. Jung, Volume 11*. New York: Pantheon, 1958.

Keane, James T. ed. *James Martin Essential Writings*. Maryknoll, New York: Orbis, 2017.

Keating, Thomas. *Intimacy with God*. New York: The Crossroad Publishing Company, 1994.

Keller, Timothy. *The Prodigal God*. New York: Riverhead, 2008.

Kim, Elizabeth. *Ten Thousand Sorrows*. St. Helens, WA: Doubleday, 2000.

Lindbergh, Ann Morrow. *Gift From The Sea*. New York: Random House, 1955.

Linn, Dennis et al. *Good Goats*. Mahwah, NJ: Paulist, 1994.

McElwee, Joshua J. "Cupich says 'Amoris Laetitia' changes how church teaches families, by learning." https://www.ncronline.org/news/theology/cupich-says-amoris-laetitia-changes-how-church-teaches-families-learning.

Merton, Thomas. *New Seeds of Contemplation*. New York: New Directions, 1961.

Miller CSB, Abp. J. Michael. *The Holy See's Teaching on Catholic Schools*. Atlanta, GA: Sophia, 2006.

Moore, Thomas. *Dark Nights of the Soul*. New York: Gotham Books, 2004.

Mulligan, CSC, James T. *A Pastor's Journal*. Toronto: Novalis, 2015.

NCR Editorial Staff, "Editorial: Evangelization requires bishops' self-examination." https://www.ncronline.org/news/vatican/editorial-evangelization-requires-bishops-self-examination.

Pope Francis. "General Audience: Saint Peter's Square, Wednesday, 19 February 2014." https://www.vatican.va/content/francesco/en/audiences/2014/documents/papa-francesco_20140219_udienza-generale.html.

———. "Holy Mass: Homily Of His Holiness Pope Francis, Air Defense Stadium, Cairo Saturday, 29 April 2017." http://www.vatican.va/content/francesco/en/homilies/2017/documents/papa-francesco_20170429_omelia-viaggioapostolico-egitto.html.

Pope Paul VI. "Declaration On The Relation Of The Church To Non-Christian Religions: Nostra Aetate." http://www.vatican.va/archive/hist_councils/ii_vatican_council/documents/vat-ii_decl_19651028_nostra-aetate_en.html.

Rohr, Richard. "Negative Capability." https://cac.org/negative-capability-2016–01–11/.

————. *What The Mystics Know*. New York: The Crossroad Publishing Company, 2015.

Rolheiser, Ronald. *Wrestling With God*. New York: Image, 2018.

Scmidt, Joseph F. *Praying Our Experiences*. Winona, MN: Saint Mary's, 1980.

Spadaro, Antonio. *A Big Heart Open To God*. New York: HarperCollins, 2013.

Swafford, Sarah. *Emotional Virtue*. Lakewood, CO: Totus Tuus, 2014.

Tobias, Michael, et al. *A Parliament of Souls*. San Francisco: KQED, 1995.

Tournier, Paul. *To Understand Each Other*. Atlanta, GA: John Knox, 1967.

USCCB. *National Directory for Catechesis*. Washington D.C., 2005.

van Breemen, SJ, Peter. *The God Who Won't Let Go*. Notre Dame, IN: Ave Maria, 2001.

Warren, Rick. *The Purpose Driven Church*. Grand Rapids, MI: Zondervan, 1995.

Westerhoff, John H III. *Will Our Children Have Faith?* Harrisburg, PA: Morehouse, 2012.

World Economic Forum, "Insight: Ideas for Change—Charter for Compassion—Karen Armstrong." https://www.youtube.com/watch?v=HttLdVug8XU.

CPSIA information can be obtained
at www.ICGtesting.com
Printed in the USA
BVHW050014211021
619364BV00007B/135